MÉXICO
GOBIERNO DE LA REPÚBLICA

SRE
CONSULADO GENERAL DE
MÉXICO EN SAN DIEGO

With the compliments of

Remedios Gómez Arnau
Consul General of Mexico in San Diego

Para lo
O-Hane,
Con mucho
Amor para
todos!
Laura.

mEXICAN

FLAVORS

A JOURNEY INSPIRED BY THE FOLKLORE AND TRADITIONS OF MEXICAN CUISINES

mEXICAN

FLAVORS

A JOURNEY INSPIRED BY THE
FOLKLORE AND TRADITIONS OF
MEXICAN CUISINES

LAURA ANHALT

PHOTOGRAPHY BY
SCOTT GABLE

Library of Congress Control Number: 2009912704
Hardcover ISBN: 978-0-615-37326-3
Softcover ISBN: 978-0-615-31099-2

Photographs copyright © 2010 by Scott Gable
(photos on pages 135, 137, 243, 250, 271, 283, 284, 287, 295 & 301 copyright © Shutterstock.com)

Book cover and interior design and layout by theBookDesigners

Edited by Carra Stratton

Introduction by Diana Anhalt

This book may be ordered by mail from the publisher.

House of Anhalt Publishing
290 Ashland Avenue
Buffalo, NY 14222-1763

DEDICATION

To my children:
Daniella, Enrique, Patrick, and Nicole

Wherever life takes you, always remember your roots.

in loving memory of:

my father, Alejandro
my uncle, Enrique
my maternal grandparents, Mauricio & Flora
my paternal grandparents, Salomon & Hanka
my dear friend, Cecilia

to Scott:

For capturing the images of my past and present through your lenses...

CONTENTS

6 DEDICATION

8 THANK YOU TO SCOTT

12 FEEDING ON THE PAST — INTRODUCTION BY MY AUNT DIANA

16 FAMILY & TRADITIONS

84 MEXICO CITY — THE BEGINNING OF OUR JOURNEY

88 THE PYRAMIDS OF TEOTIHUACÁN

104 THE DAY OF THE DEAD

132 ANGANGUEO — MICHOACÁN

160 REAL DE CATORCE, SAN LUIS POTOSÍ

174 GUANAJUATO

FROM MY TABLE TO YOURS

    214 – Tacos

    232 – Salsas

    248 – Rice & other sides

    268 – Main Dishes

    288 – Sweet Delicacies & Desserts

314 GLOSSARY

316 RECIPE INDEX

322 ACKNOWLEDGEMENTS

FEEDING ON
THE PAST

FEEDING ON THE PAST

Introduction
by my aunt Diana Anhalt

I am not the least bit surprised that my niece, Laura Anhalt, would write a book concerned— to a great extent— about food. After all, our life as a family often came together around a table. That table could stand in a patio, her mother's dining room, or in a restaurant, but you could be sure that the table would be loaded down with food: towers of pancakes, slices of watermelon, glass dishes filled with ceviche, tureens of tortilla soup, brisket, strawberry short cake.

Sunday was restaurant day. Almost every Sunday from the time they were toddlers in strollers, Laura along with her brothers and cousins, my two children, would lunch in one Mexico City restaurant or another. With her grandparents on her father's side we might go to *Bavaria*, a German place, at one time frequented by Mexican writer Carlos Fuentes. Panoramic mountain views lined

the walls, and dented metal ashtrays and sugar bowls sat atop frayed red and white checkered table cloths. At their end of the table the kids would be suspiciously silent until we were roused by a loud crash. They had been constructing pyramids with the butter plate, the bread basket, the empty upside down glasses, and the salt

and pepper shakers. At some point the structure would collapse and the adults, immersed in conversation, would leap from their seats. But once plates heaped with *Wiener Rostbraten*, red cabbage, schnitzel and strudel appeared, the table would fall silent.

There were more distractions to keep the children occupied at the *Caballo Bayo* Restaurant: Behind a glass enclosure visible from our table, women slapped tortilla dough between the palms of their hands and the kids would stand in front and watch. There was a playground, as well, and sometimes Laura's father hired mariachis to serenade us with *La Bikina, Cama de Piedra, La Llorona*. Here the table would spread from one wall to another in order to accommodate a grandfather, grandmother, aunts, uncles and plenty of cousins. It would be laden with salsas— *tomatillo, habanera, Mexicana*— with *bolillos* and tortillas, of course. And the food would keep coming: *tacos sudados*, chicken in *mole, chiles rellenos,* and *sábanas* -beef pounded so thin it overlapped the edge of the plate. Consuming one meal could easily take three hours; and one day, when we were through, Laura's father, Alejandro, my husband's twin brother, stretched and said: "You know, what I love about this place is that you can always eat lightly." (We thought he was kidding. He wasn't.)

On Saturdays we often met at Laura's mother's house for lunch. I generally bought a dessert, a date and

nut torte or an apple cake from *Bondy's*, my favorite bakery. We would sit in the family room munching on pumpkin seeds or pieces of goats' cheese in *salsa verde* while the children organized theatrical productions, dressing up in cast off clothing and sometimes donning masks or smearing their faces with makeup and elaborating dialogue. These they would perform in the garden after we had lunched on Mexican rice and *carne asada,* barbecued on the grill, along with scallions and little green chiles.

But family gatherings weren't restricted to Mexico City. Weekends were often spent at Laura's family's home in the resort town of Cuernavaca, just over an hour away. Although the children looked forward to swimming, spending the nights together, and just having more breathing space, one of the highlights was Flora, the cook, who could prepare a breakfast of scrambled eggs *a la Mexicana*, refried beans and cinnamon french toast for eighteen, all of us eating in shifts. I remember glorious, sunny days revolving around three-course meals.

Every morning after swimming for hours the kids would emerge from the pool and, still dripping wet, head to the terrace for a snack consisting of carrot, cucumber and *jícama* sticks. They'd top them off with chile powder and salt and bathe them in lime juice. However, we started to notice that, on return to Mexico

City; they all had brown streaks on their faces and stomachs. It wasn't until Laura's mother took them to the dermatologist that we realized the streaks resulted from wiping their hands dripping in lime juice on their bodies and then being exposed to the sun. So, this experience marked them—both literally and figuratively.

We were all marked by our times together, by a past suffused with a kind of glow. Certainly these events left their mark on Laura for whom moments with family and food have become moments to treasure, moments worthy of a book.

—*Diana Anhalt*

FAMILY AND TRADITIONS

FAMILY AND TRADITIONS

to Sylvia, my mother
"el hambre se quita, pero el sentimiento nunca"- dicho mexicano

What a wonderful thing, memories! My strongest ones seem to always revolve around family and food. I grew up in Mexico City as a child of Mexican nationals and a grandchild of European immigrants. In my particular case, the stork who delivered me was forced to make an emergency landing in Los Angeles, California granting me the privilege of holding dual nationalities.

My passion for good food started at a very early age as I spent many hours of my days immersed in the smells and flavors of my mother's kitchen. The household cooks would work tirelessly from dusk to dawn preparing both Mexican and International selections.

My parents had a friendly way of persuading my brothers and I to try all kinds of foods even at a very young age. So sure enough, by the time I was 7 years old, I was well on my way to enjoying culinary rarities such as iguana, snails, grasshoppers, corn fungus, chocolate covered ants, caviar, and other eccentric foodstuffs.

My father, Alejandro, his twin brother Mauricio and their older brother Enrique were first generation Mexican born. My grandmother, Hanka, was Polish

and my grandfather, Salomon, was Austro-Hungarian. They moved to Mexico City sometime between the First and Second World Wars.

My grandfather had a kind and peaceful spirit. He was a calm and quiet man, good natured, elegant in his demeanor and as polite as I know anyone to be. Everyone who knew him referred to him being gentle as a dame, and a noble man.

I hold tight and cherish every memory we built together. It was fun to take a stroll with him through the park and to feed the ducks or row a boat. He taught me how to play badminton, backgammon and chess. But what I loved the most was engaging with him in what my mother used to call *junk food crimes*. After my grandmother passed away, my brothers, cousins and I would sometimes spend the night at his apartment over the weekends to keep him company. He would gather us all at the kitchen table and feed us *halah* bread topped with fresh sour cream and salt. He would also prepare a special liquid concoction that consisted of mixing together a variety of soft drinks such as ginger ale, orange crush and whatever other kind he had available. For some reason, I have never liked drinking soda so I didn't care much for that special drink. I did, however, manage to gulp it down every single time and never said a word, fearing I might hurt his feelings.

Even though we were very close, I can't say I know much about my grandfather's life before his arrival to Mexico City.

I tried knocking on the doors of his past many times, always trying to find the perfect setting or mood for him to talk -and me to listen, but every time I approached him with questions, he kindly refused to engage in those particular conversations. My father and uncles, if they knew, didn't speak of it either. The only significant piece of information I have came through my mother, who by asking around, learned that he sadly lost his brothers and sisters to the Holocaust; all except one. His brother, Pinkas, also abandoned Europe before the Second World War and raised his family in Israel, Palestine at the time.

My grandfather battled with Alzheimer's disease for the last years of his life and passed away shortly before I got married. It was a tremendous loss for me but, I feel grateful to have known him, to have loved him, and for the life lessons he taught me.

I have a clear picture in my mind of what my grandmother Hanka looked like and the kind of person she used to be, but I'm afraid it's not exactly a memory based on time spent together. She succumbed to a violent cancer when I was very young. My parents, grandfather, and aunts and uncles kept her memory alive by talking about her, showing us pictures and preparing food from her collection of strictly European dishes.

I learned that her parents died when she and her sisters were very young. They were all sent to different

family members to continue to be raised. The aunt and uncle who raised my grandmother provided her with a formidable education; as a matter of fact, she studied to become a mathematics teacher and taught for a couple of years in her native Poland before moving to Mexico. She was also taught to speak *Esperanto*, a politically unbiased language that is spoken by people who are internationally minded and concerned about social justice. Sadly, not all of her sisters had the same luck. My great-aunt Rita –the youngest of the sisters- endured many hardships and suffered mistreatments by the family members who raised her.

Eventually, my grandmother and her sisters reunited in Mexico City after many years of being apart. She and my great-aunt Rita remained the closest. Although my great-aunt Rita was married and wanted a child passionately, she was never able to conceive one of her own. So my grandmother, acknowledging her pain, allowed her to raise the boys' right along side her; the boys in turn loved her dearly and considered her a second mother. Rita, I still remember her vividly. She passed away roughly a year before my grandfather did.

Of what I have heard and tasted in my past, my grandmother was an excellent cook. My mother made every effort to learn how to prepare her dishes, a skill which she learned to master quite well. She would joyously prepare my grandmother's recipes when my father's family came over for lunch or dinner or on certain special occasions. She would receive wonderful critiques and words of praise from everyone-all except my father- who although recognized that the food had turned out exquisitely, firmly believed no one could cook as well as his mother.

Even though my writings are in essence related to Mexican cuisines, the way that I cook and develop my recipes these days is greatly influenced by the different types of food I grew up eating; for that reason, it would not make much sense to exclude the recipes of some of the European dishes I learned to treasure, those that so strongly helped shape my culinary memories.

CHOPPED LIVER

HIGADITOS PICADOS

Ingredients:

2.2 lbs of chicken liver
5 white onions, sliced
1/2 lb of butter or solid chicken fat
8 eggs, hard boiled (reserve 2 eggs to decorate serving platter)
1 cube or packet of chicken bouillon (optional)
1 small tomato (optional)
Salt & pepper to taste

TO PREPARE:

Rinse and clean the chicken liver in cold water and drain. Set aside.

Melt the butter or chicken fat in a large frying pan over medium heat and add the sliced onions. Season them with salt and pepper or with the cube of chicken bouillon and fry them until they turn dark and crispy. Remove about ½ a cup of the fried onions from the frying pan and set them aside to later use as garnish.

Add the chicken liver to the onions in the frying pan and cook until well done, but not dry. Transfer the chicken liver and onions to a food processor along with 6 of the boiled eggs and chop them until all of the ingredients are well mixed. The desired consistency of the final dish is up to the individual preparing it. It can be anywhere from lumpy to somewhat smooth. Adjust the seasoning with salt & pepper if needed.

TO SERVE:

Arrange the chopped liver on a serving platter, preferably crystal, and garnish with the fried onions. If desired, decorate the platter with thin slices of hard boiled egg and a tomato carved to resemble a flower. Serve with wheat crackers or small pieces of toast.

HERRING SALAD

ARENQUE EN ENSALADA

· Ingredients:
1 jar of whole herring in cream sauce
1/2 jar of whole herring in oil
1 yellow apple, chopped
1/4 cup of sour cream
Curly parsley, enough to garnish (optional)
Multicolored olives, enough to garnish (optional)

TO PREPARE:

Reserve 3 pieces of whole herring to garnish the salad.

Transfer the herring in oil to a small mesh strainer to rid it from the excess oil.

Once the oil has drained, put the herring in oil, the herring in cream sauce, the chopped apple, and the sour cream in the food processor and mix to the desired consistency.

TO SERVE:

Arrange the herring salad in a serving platter or dish. Decorate it by placing the slices of whole herring on top, and with the curly parsley leaves and/or multicolored olives. Serve alongside crackers or small pieces of rye toast.

GRANDMA HANKA'S EGG SALAD

ENSALADA DE HUEVO DE LA ABUELA HANKA

Ingredients:
12 to 14 eggs, hard boiled
1/2 cup of celery, very finely chopped
1/2 cup of scallions, finely chopped, including the green parts
1/4 cup of pickles, finely chopped
4 tablespoons of mayonnaise
1 tablespoon of sour cream
1 tablespoon of Dijon mustard
1/2 teaspoon of paprika
1/2 teaspoon of dried basil
Pickles, sliced (to garnish)
1 small tomato (to garnish)
Salt & pepper to taste

TO PREPARE:

Chop the eggs or coarsely mash them with a fork. Transfer the chopped eggs into a bowl and add the rest of the ingredients. Mix well until all of the ingredients are perfectly combined. Adjust the seasoning with salt & pepper as needed.

TO SERVE:

Transfer the egg salad to a serving platter and decorate it with sliced pickles and the tomato in slices or carved to resemble a flower.

VIENNESE SAUSAGE AND POTATO SALAD

ENSALADA DE SALCHICHA VIENESA Y PAPA

Serves 6

Ingredients:
4 veal sausages, cooked and skinned
4 potatoes, oven baked and peeled
1 large purple onion, sliced
1 teaspoon of dry dill
Olive oil, as desired
White vinegar, as desired
Salt & pepper to taste

TO PREPARE:

Wrap the raw potatoes individually in tin foil and bake them until soft. Remove them from the oven and set aside to cool at room temperature.

Put the sausages in a saucepan, cover them with water and cook until done. Once cooked, drain the water using a colander and allow the sausages to cool at room temperature.

When the potatoes are cold enough to handle, peel off the skin and immediately slice them to obtain ¼ of an inch thick wedges.

When the sausages are cold enough, peel the skin off and slice them into ¼ of an inch thick wedges.

TO ASSEMBLE:

Place the potato and sausage wedges directly in the serving platter. Add the dry dill, vinegar and olive oil to your taste, and season it lightly with salt and pepper. Toss gently to prevent the potatoes from falling apart.

SOUR PICKLES
PEPINOS AGRIOS

Ingredients:
24 baby cucumbers, whole
8 cups of water
6 garlic cloves, whole
4 cups of white wine vinegar
4 serrano chiles, whole
Whole black peppercorns
Dry bay leaves
Coarse salt to taste

TO PREPARE:

Boil the water with the peppercorns, bay leaves, salt, vinegar, garlic, and the chiles. Allow the liquid to boil for about 15 minutes, remove from heat, and let it cool until it becomes lukewarm.

Meanwhile, in a clean large glass jar or a couple of smaller ones, arrange the baby cucumbers over-lapping them in such a way that they rest tightly against each other, until the whole jar is full.

Add the lukewarm liquid into the jar. Taste and adjust the seasoning if needed by adding more salt or vinegar. Close the jar tightly with its lid and place it in the refrigerator. The pickles will be ready in three to four days.

The pickles keep well for about a month provided they are refrigerated.

SWEET PURPLE CABBAGE

COL MORADA

Serves 6

Ingredients:
1 large purple cabbage
1/2 white onion, finely chopped
1/4 lb of butter
4 tablespoons of all purpose flour
6 tablespoons of brown sugar
1/2 cup of white vinegar
Water, enough to cover the cabbage while it cooks
Salt to taste

TO PREPARE:

Cut the cabbage into thin slices, rinse under cold water and let drain.

In a large frying pan melt the butter over medium heat. Add the chopped onion and when it is golden brown, add the flour and stir. Cook until the mixture turns a light brown. At this point, add the purple cabbage and sear it over high heat until it begins to brown, for about 5 to 7 minutes. Stir constantly to prevent the cabbage from burning.

Once all of the cabbage is uniformly seared, add enough water to cover all of it and then add the brown sugar, vinegar and salt to taste. Stir well and reduce the heat to low, cover with a lid, and let it cook for about 1 ½ hours. Check it from time to time, stir it to prevent burning and if needed, adjust the seasoning by adding more salt or brown sugar as you go. Cook until the cabbage is soft, but not mushy. The outcome of this dish should be sweet and sour.

Alternatively, you can prepare this same recipe with green or white cabbage. The name of this dish is choucrout, also known as sauerkraut. You can modify the recipe by adding less brown sugar and adding a couple of dry bay leaves and black peppercorns. Also, it will require less cooking time because choucrout is usually firmer.

TO SERVE:

This recipe is a side dish to be served with Polish sausages and is also good to serve alongside plain baked potatoes.

CHICKEN IN SWEET AND SOUR APRICOT SAUCE

POLLO EN SALSA AGRIDULCE DE CHABACANO

Ingredients:
2 whole chickens, cut into pieces (legs, thighs, breasts)
1 can of Campbell's onion soup
1 garlic clove
1 small jar of honey
1 large jar of apricot marmalade
Maggi sauce to taste
Worcestershire sauce to taste
Pineapple juice, as needed
Salt & pepper to taste

TO PREPARE:

Preheat oven to 300°F.

Rinse the chickens, skin them, and cut them into pieces. Place them on a glass Pyrex dish or roasting pan with a lid. Salt and pepper them lightly. Set aside.

Put the can of onion soup, the garlic clove, the marmalade, the honey, Worchestershire and Maggi saucesin the blender jar. Mix until well combined. Mix until all of the ingredients are well combined.

Pour the apricot sauce over the chicken pieces and bake for 2 to 3 hours depending on your oven's efficiency. Check constantly to make sure that the chicken is not burning and that the sauce is not drying up. Baste the pieces from time to time to ensure even coverage. If you find that the sauce is becoming too dry and sticky, add some pineapple juice to thin out the sauce.

CARROTS AND PRUNES - TZIMES

TZIMES–ZANAHORIAS CON CIRUELAS

Serves 6

Ingredients:
1 bag of baby carrots, whole
1 small bag of prunes, whole
1/4 cup of white onion, very finely chopped
1/4 lb of butter
1/4 cup of honey
1/4 cup dark brown sugar
Sea salt to taste

TO PREPARE:

Cook the baby carrots until soft, but not mushy, by putting them in a saucepan with boiling water. Drain the cooked carrots and set aside.

In the same saucepan you used to cook the carrots, melt the butter over medium heat. Fry the chopped onion and season it lightly with salt. Add the cooked baby carrots, prunes, honey, and dark brown sugar. Stir until well mixed and the sugar and the honey have softened, and are well incorporated with the rest of the ingredients, for about 5 minutes. Serve immediately.

TO SERVE:

Tzimes are a great accompaniment for chicken or beef. It is a very popular and simple side dish served during the Jewish holidays.

My father was a certified public accountant and a factory owner. Nevertheless, those who knew him well would playfully joke around saying he was a frustrated chef. A joke indeed because as hard as I try, I cannot remember my father cooking - except maybe at the grill. What I do remember is him in the kitchen, hovering over pots and pans with a tasting spoon in hand, always eager to taste and provide his opinion.

He might not have been a chef but he was, unquestionably, a food and drink connoisseur. He enjoyed all types of foods and was just as happy eating *tacos* or *esquites* –corn off the cob -prepared by street vendors and drinking *pulque* – a fermented alcoholic beverage- out of a plastic cup at the door step of an old and rustic cantina, as he was dining at a five star restaurant enjoying gourmet dishes and drinking some of the finest wines available.

Whenever asked about what his favorite foods were, he would answer: "Without a doubt, simple, down-to-earth Mexican dishes are my favorite." This answer would perplex me since he was notorious for eating fare that I would not regard as simple or even down-to-earth. His food selections could be rather exotic and sometimes, truly unappealing.

His love for food was not confined by geographical borders. He was an enthusiastic traveler and a firm believer that the only way to immerse yourself in new cultures and to absorb them all in is to eat the traditional foods of the regions and shop at the local markets. To this he held true whether we were traveling within the Mexican Republic or in far away countries.

From the time I was an older teen until we could no longer go places together because of his frail health, if we happened to be in Mexico City for the weekend, we would invariably embark on a day-long excruciating food buying expedition to one of the most impressive food markets in the world: *el Mercado de San Juan*.

The *San Juan* Market has been around since times immemorial and is considered a part of Mexican folklore. It is a place where the stallholders feel great pride and honor to be able to sell

their goods at such a historical and privileged location. As a customer, it can be rather overwhelming, but nowhere else in the city can you shop around for the rarity and diversity of foods and items found there. Not only can you find the best and largest selections of fresh fruits, vegetables, creams, and cheeses in the city; you are also able to find foods and ingredients of pre-Hispanic origins including edible insects of all sorts, exotic meat selections such as iguana, armadillo, goat, snake, frog and even lion, as well as a vast selection of ocean edibles such as shark, octopus, gigantic

shrimp and squid, swordfish, catfish, sea urchin, and algae. You can also find some of the finest cooking oils in the world and other international, hard to find delicacies from around the globe.

My father and I would scour the whole place, going from vendor stall to vendor stall, looking for the best and most exotic finds of the day. We would mainly buy fruits and vegetables, cream, cheese, eggs, oils, herbs, dried chiles and beans, coffee, and seafood or meats depending on what he was craving.

Before heading home and calling it a day, we would stop by the prepared

foods section where we would grab something to eat and drink-standing up, as it is customary, delighting ourselves with seafood *tostadas* galore -crab being my personal favorite- and drinking *aguas frescas y jugos,* fresh juices and sweet flavored water such as cucumber, *jamaica* – hibiscus flower water- and *horchata* – rice water.

My father took these food buying expeditions very seriously. He would hand pick each of the fruit and vegetable pieces individually and would return home very proud of his varieties and selections; so much so in fact, that when we sat down for lunch or dinner and someone commented on what a fine avocado they had just opened or what a sweet mango they had just had as a dessert, he would brag and say: "why...I picked it myself!" If by some unfortunate twist of fate one of the fruits or vegetables once opened was less than perfect, he would pin the blame on the fruit vendor and sometimes on me. No one ever took any offense, much less me, because as pitiable as his comments might have been, they were actually quite funny.

CRAB TOSTADAS

TOSTADAS DE CANGREJO

Serves 3

Ingredients:

6 corn tortillas
1/2 cup of vegetable oil, to fry the tortillas
2 heaping tablespoons of light olive oil
1 lb of crab meat, cooked (ideally, use real crab but imitation crab is acceptable)
2 serrano chiles, cut in thin rounds
2 ripe avocados, 1 cut into cubes and the other one sliced
1 large tomato, diced in small pieces and without seeds
1/2 small onion, very finely chopped
1/2 cup of cilantro or parsley, finely chopped
1/2 teaspoon of dried oregano
3 limes, squeezed
Salt & pepper to taste

TO PREPARE:

Heat the oil in a small, deep saucepan. Make sure the oil is hot before frying. Deep fry 1 tortilla at a time until it becomes crispy and golden, turning it about every half a minute or so. Use metal tongs or a spatula with slits to aid you in the process. Transfer the fried tortillas onto a plate covered with paper towels to rid them of the excess oil. Set aside.

Meanwhile, shred the cooked crab meat with your hands into a large mixing bowl. Add the olive oil, the juice from three limes, the onion, the cilantro or parsley, tomato, cubed avocado, serrano chiles, and oregano. Adjust the seasoning by adding salt & pepper as needed. Mix well and set aside.

TO SERVE:

Pat-dry the tortillas and place two on each plate. Top each tortilla with about ¼ of a cup of the crab salad and put one slice of avocado on top of each tostada.

CORN OFF THE COB

ESQUITES

Serves 4

Esquites are corn kernels served in disposable plastic cups that are prepared with lime juice, salt, mayonnaise, and powdered chile peppers (such as cayenne). There is nothing better than to eat something healthy and hearty when you are on the go. No fuss, no mess and a lot of satisfaction!

To prepare esquites you will need 2 large, fresh, uncooked corn cobs for each person you are serving it to.

Ingredients:
8 corn cobs, the bigger the kernels the better
Mayonnaise, as needed
4 limes, squeezed
Chile piquín, tajín, miguelito or substitute with powdered cayenne pepper
Salt to taste

TO PREPARE:

Peel and clean the corn cobs and put them in boiling water. Allow them to cook and when the kernels become tender, remove them from the water and let drain.

Cut the kernels off of the cob by using a fine pairing knife. Make sure to have the corn standing and well held to prevent it from slipping.

Put all the corn kernels in a small bowl; add the lime juice and mix well to incorporate. Add the mayonnaise to your liking and adjust the seasoning with salt.

TO SERVE:

Serve in individual transparent plastic cups (or on plates) and sprinkle them with cayenne pepper or your choice of powdered hot peppers depending on your personal level of heat comfort.

Don't shy away from using chili peppers; they bring great taste to a healthy snack.

RICE WATER
AGUA DE HORCHATA

Ingredients:
2 cups of white rice
4 cups of hot water, to soak the rice
2 cups of evaporated milk
4 cups of cold water
4 cinnamon sticks, toasted
Cinnamon powder, to garnish
White cane sugar, as needed
Ice cubes (optional)

TO PREPARE:

Soak the rice in 4 cups of hot water for 3 hours.

Meanwhile, break up the cinnamon stick with your hands and place the pieces on a small skillet over medium heat to toast them until you can smell the slight aroma of the cinnamon being released.

Drain the rice and immediately grind it with the toasted cinnamon and the milk, by using a blender or food processor. Try to get it as smooth as you can. Strain the rice milk through a fine mesh colander directly into the serving pitcher, and dilute it with 4 cups of cold water; add the ice cubes, sugar as needed and mix well. Sprinkle the powdered cinnamon on top.

HIBISCUS FLOWER WATER

AGUA DE JAMAICA

Serves 6

Ingredients:

2 loose cups of dried hibiscus flower, easily available
at specialty food stores

10 cups of cold water

Sugar, as needed

Ice cubes (optional)

TO PREPARE:

Bring 5 of the cups of water to a rolling boil over high heat.

Rinse the hibiscus flowers to rid them of impurities and add them into the boiling water. Reduce the heat to medium, cover, and allow the flowers to boil in the water for 10 minutes. Remove from the heat and set aside to cool, about 30 minutes.

Strain the hibiscus water into the serving pitcher and dilute it with the remaining 5 cups of cold water. Add the ice cubes, sugar as needed, and mix well.

CUCUMBER WATER

AGUA DE PEPINO

Serves 6

Ingredients:
2 cucumbers, cubed
6 cups of water, cold
3 limes, their juice
7 mint leaves
Sugar, as needed
Ice cubes (optional)

TO PREPARE:

Wash and cube the cucumbers leaving the skin and seeds intact.

Transfer the cucumber pieces to the blender, add 2 cups of water and blend very well until you achieve a smooth purée. Stop the blender, add 1 more cup of water, the lime juice, 1 mint leaf and blend again until liquefied. Stop the blender once more and add 1 more cup of water and blend for an additional minute on high.

Strain the cucumber water into the serving pitcher and dilute it with the remaining 2 cups of cold water. Add the ice cubes, sugar as needed, and mix well. Put ice cubes and 1 mint leaf in every glass to be served.

Alternatively, you may wish to use this same recipe with strawberries, melon or honeydew

WATERMELON WATER

AGUA FRESCA DE SANDÍA

Serves 6

Ingredients:
4 cups of watermelon, cubed
4 cups of cold water
Sugar, as needed

TO PREPARE:

Put 2 cups of the watermelon with 2 cups of water in the blender and mix until completely liquefied. Strain it directly into the serving pitcher and repeat the process with the rest of the watermelon and water. Add sugar as needed.

I know a lot more about my mother's side of the family than what I know about my father's side. Both my grandparents lived well into my adult life. They were there while I was growing up, when I got married and when I became a mother. They even got a chance to enjoy being great-grandparents to my children for a few years past toddler-hood.

My grandfather, Mauricio, was born in the city of Vilna, Lithuania, to a middle-class family in the early 1900's. He was the second of three children born to my great-grandparents Benjamin and Miriam. By his own recollection, they lived quite a comfortable life up until the Russian invasion of Poland that happened between the years of 1917 and 1918. These were times of war and Europe's situation was rapidly deteriorating. Around 1925, his father left Lithuania in hopes of finding better fortune in Mexico, which at that time was a young developing country. He wanted to bring them all but couldn't guarantee their sustenance and left his wife and children behind until he knew for sure that he could provide a stable home for them in Mexico.

Due to the scarcity of food and with his father gone, my grandfather began to work at the age of 13 to help provide for his family. As soon as his father was able to send money back home, their conditions improved dramatically, and in 1929, after 3 long years of being apart, the whole family finally reunited in the city of Puebla.

Upon their arrival to Mexico, my grandfather's first job was to help his father sell clothes from door to door. Unbeknownst to him at that time, this would be the detonator that sparked forth the clothing empire he eventually built. He was a hard working man with a good head for business and, little by little, he began establishing fine clothing stores for men and tailor shops in Puebla, and then Mexico City. He worked them with his brother Samuel, and his brother-in-law Salomon. Along the way, the three of them developed different interests and after 38 years of partnership, they parted ways. My grandfather went on to become one of the best known names in the men's clothing design and manufacturing industry in Mexico.

Aside from being hardworking, my grandfather was a kindhearted philanthropist. He had a strong sense of community and wanted to provide his children with the many opportunities that he did not have while growing up. His generous donations to the Jewish community in Mexico were used to help build Temple Beth-el, the Jewish Community Center and to buy land to be used as a cemetery. He also provided scholarships to Jewish boys and girls whose parents couldn't afford to send them to private school.

A few days prior to his death my grandfather said to me out of the blue: "you know, tochter (daughter, in German), I don't believe in god..." His statement surprised me; after all, you could find him every Sabbath and Jewish holiday sitting in the same chair at the temple -week in, week out, year in, year out. But I wasn't shocked. I knew of the hard times and misery he had witnessed and endured through his life and so I asked him: "Why then, did you invest all your time and money into helping build the Jewish community in Mexico? "Because..." – he answered – "I wanted to give the children a sense of faith and belonging; the two things I never had." That was the kind of man he was and the legacy he left behind.

His favorite food item was fish. Any kind, you name it, he liked it. His favorite breakfast consisted of a toasted bagel with a plentiful dab of cream cheese

topped off with smoked salmon, chopped hard boiled eggs, pickled capers, and lime juice. My grandmother made sure there was at least one serving of fish per day available to him whether it was in the form of an appetizer, a main dish or even as a mid-day snack. He loved to munch on salted crackers and herring -pickled or in a cream sauce- salted cod, anchovies; smoked mackerel, and canned sardines. He would eat with great gusto a delicious appetizer dish that consisted of red snapper in a creamy white sauce topped off with bread crumbs and parmesan cheese baked in large ceramic shells; and a tin foil baked fish in a delectable tequila-chipotle sauce prepared by the cooks of my grandparents' home under the ever watchful eye of my grandmother who believed that she, herself, was not a good cook.

My grandmother, Flora, was the only one of my grandparents who was first generation Mexican born. She was born in Mexico City in the 1920's to my great-grandfather Marcos, who was originally Polish and my great-grandmother, Miriam who was from Berlin, Germany. The love my great-grandparents had for each other and the life adventures they shared together were remarkable and truly worthy of a Shakespeare play.

The tale tells that my great-grandfather was born in rural Poland at the turn of the 19th century. He was born into poverty to a very large, but loving family. They earned their keep processing animal skins to be sold for clothing manufacturing, horse saddles and home furniture. They ran the business out of the yard of their humble home. My great-grandfather was very sensitive to the deep, penetrating, pungent smells of the dead animal skins and to the chemicals used to blanch them. Fearing he could never stick around to learn the tricks of the trade, he left his home empty-handed at the age of 12, never to return again.

He gallivanted from place to place working odd jobs for food and shelter, always looking for the right spot to eventually call home. He made it to Budapest, Hungary where he lived with a photographer who took him under his wing and mentored him into the photography business. He excelled at re-touching the pictures, a thing that came almost naturally to him. He was a very talented artist, even though at the time he wasn't yet aware of it.

While in Budapest, he met a Countess who, although older in age, fell deeply in love with him and asked him to marry her. Since he was very young at the time, he didn't feel ready to commit to the lifestyle he would inherit from a Countess and once more, gathered his adventurous spirit, his few belongings and left Budapest for good. Shortly thereafter in 1917, he was recruited by the Polish army and forcibly returned to his native land to serve his country during the First World War. Not wanting to have a hand at war because he believed in peace, he deserted his troops and skipped town.

He found refuge in Germany and moved from town to town until he finally landed a job in Berlin with a local photographer. Because he was young and considered a novice in the trade, he was only allowed to do the picture touch-ups and some odd jobs around the photography studio. One day, he was handed the photograph of a gorgeous young woman and knew he had to meet her. He decided to follow the person who picked it up to see where it would lead him. He stood outside the walls of an impressive mansion, patiently waiting to see if this beautiful young lady would somehow miraculously appear, for his heart ached to meet her.

On the flip side, my great-grandmother, Miriam, was born into privilege also at the turn of the 19th century. She lived with her father who was a Rabbi, and her siblings in Berlin. Her mother was ill with tuberculosis and was forced to live in quarantine for many years of her life in a location within the Black Forest. Up until that point, my great-grandmother's life had been relatively normal and uneventful. Also, as it was customary of the Jewish traditions back then, her marriage had already been arranged to a nice young man who was studying to become a Rabbi, just like her father.

One day, she felt compelled to approach her balcony and look out on to the street. And there he was, a stunning young man staring up directly at her. Her heart melted, and she knew in an instant that she had to meet him. She asked one of the younger maids in her household to let her wear some of her clothing so that she could leave the house undetected and meet this young man. And so they came to know each other; and every night thereafter, my great-grandmother would change her clothes and leave the house to go be with the love of her life. Fearing they might get caught and that her father would force her in to marriage in retaliation, they decided to get married in secret. They got married with a Rabbi under the Jewish law since my great-grandmother was very religious and wouldn't have it any other way.

This was sometime around the year 1918 and the situation in Europe was dire. Once more, my great-grandfather's adventurous spirit led him to look for a better life, but this time, somewhere in the Americas. He could not afford to take his young bride with him so he set sail without her, promising to come back for her as soon as he possibly could. For the next two years, she waited and kept her marriage a secret. Finally, he was able to send for her; and on the evening of a very cold autumn night in 1920, without bidding farewell to anyone, she set sail towards the port of Veracruz, Mexico as her final destination and like my great-grandfather before her, never to return again.

My great-grandfather set up his photography shop and art studio as soon as he arrived in Mexico City. This trade fed him and his family well for the whole rest of his life. He was an excellent photographer and became a famous portrait painter. For my great-grandparents, Mexico City was the final destination in their continent-country-city-hopping journey and the place where they eventually set their roots.

All in all, my great-grandparents had four children. Their first born, a boy, died at birth; then came my grandmother, Flora; and years after, her sister Estella, who died of polio at the tender age of 12. And then the youngest one, my uncle Willy, who although much younger than the rest, has also unfortunately passed away. They had 8 grandchildren, and by the time their lives ended, 6 great-grandchildren. When I was born, my great-grandfather painted a carnival clown in oil on canvas as a birth-gift that hung in my bedroom until the day I left home; it is a piece of art I truly treasure and has likewise decorated my children's room's at different times of their lives. Most of his paintings now hang in the homes of our family members as a testimony to his talent, his love and respect for nature, the love he felt for his wife, and his remarkable adventurous sprit.

My grandmother, their daughter, was a woman of unnatural beauty. Outwardly, she was simply stunning. She was witty and fun and had a fantastic sense of humor. No wonder why just 15 days after having met her, my grandfather asked for her hand in marriage. They were married in 1942 when she was 17 and he was 29. They bought a home in the city of Puebla but soon thereafter, they relocated to Mexico City because my grandmother longed to be near her parents in the city where she grew up. Since the day they became husband and wife, my grandfather devoted his life to satisfying my grandmother's every wish and desire.

Together they had four children: Jack, Sylvia, Eduardo, and Mónica. My grandmother became a mother at a very early age and my mother, Sylvia, made her a very young grandmother as well. Because of this, I was lucky to have such a vibrant and fun grandmother. I absolutely adored her. She was my friend and my confidant. She taught me all about secrets and together, we had many. She educated me in the fine art of listening and observing... but not telling. Although I recognize this was mainly a way for her to manipulate certain situations to her advantage, I learned to be a sensitive and discreet person, a trait that has proven valuable in my life.

One of our secrets was her smoking. She wasn't supposed to smoke because she had emphysema and several different types of cancers throughout her life. She was banned from smoking, but around me, she knew her secret was safe. Another secret was our weekly binging episodes at *Sanborns*- a historical restaurant that as the years have gone by, has unfortunately lowered its food and service standards. I believe she must have also had some sort of a food restriction because every Thursday, right between lunch and dinner, we would go to *Sanborns* and indulge ourselves with the same food every single time: *Enchiladas Suizas* and refried beans, freshly made corn tortilla chips with salt and salsas, and for dessert, we'd share a great big chocolate fudge ice-cream sundae.

As a family, we would spend some of our weekends at my grandparent's vacation home in the city of Cuernavaca, a short distance away from Mexico City. The gardener, Herminio, and the cook, Flora, were a married couple who lived with their children in their own private home within the premises of our property. Flora, who shared the same first name with my grandmother, was a spectacular cook. Without a doubt, she's had a tremendous impact in the way I prepare most of my recipes.

Since food always held center stage in my family, these weekend escapades were full of it. The mornings would begin with everyone getting served breakfast at different time intervals just because we all woke up at different times. The table would be set for the amount of people visiting that weekend, anywhere between 12 and 32. Flora had at least two different kinds of salsas going to prepare eggs any-style, and the table was lined with pitchers of freshly squeezed orange juice, milk, sweet bread baskets, sliced fruit platters, and 1-serving boxes of cereal to make sure she satisfied everyone's eating desires. Not in the mood for eggs? Pancakes or French toast cravings that morning? No problem, just ask!

At around noon, Flora would march out towards the swimming pool area where we were all hanging out and she would line the patio tables with pitchers of water and juices, vegetable and fruit platters, bowls of potato chips and fried tortillas, dips and dipping sauces, and a myriad of hot sauces like Tabasco, Buffalo and chamoy salsa (recipe on pages

204-205), powdered chiles, and a good amount of halved limes from our fruit grove so everybody could prepare their own snacks.

The dip I drooled over and still do, is Flora's onion dip. And then, of course, there was lunch. Always served at the huge stone tables in the open terrace. We kids ate first at around 3:00pm. The mothers and nannies would keep watch making sure we behaved well and didn't forget our proper table manners, but we would not have dessert until the grownups had finished their lunch, at which time we would all seek out our parents' laps for they provided a comfy seating area while savoring our dessert.

Dinners were usually light and consisted of hot chocolate, coffee, sweet breads, and enormous platters of cold cuts, vegetables, cheeses and spreads to make our own sandwiches.

I don't know the whereabouts of Flora and Herminio these days. After my grandparents passed away, the house in Cuernavaca was sold as per stipulated in their will to a gentleman who just so happens to be one of the franchise owners of McDonald's. So the house was sold and a portion of our beautiful vacation property, the one where we grew up swimming and playing tennis, where we ran around as kids' collecting sweet mangoes, limes and avocados from the trees, was pitifully turned into a McDonald's restaurant.

FLORA'S ONION AND CILANTRO DIP

DIP DE CEBOLLA Y CILANTRO ESTILO FLORA

Ingredients:
1 oz package of Philadelphia cream cheese, softened
8 oz of sour cream
1 tablespoon of chicken bouillon, powdered
1/2 tablespoon of crackled black pepper
1/2 tablespoon of Worcestershire sauce
1 small red onion, minced
1 small white onion, chopped finely and fried
1/2 tablespoon of olive oil, to fry the onion
1/2 cup of fresh cilantro, minced

TO PREPARE:

Chop the white onion and fry it until crispy and brown. Set aside.

Mash the softened cream cheese and sour cream together with a fork and add the rest of the ingredients including the fried onion, mixing well, until all of the ingredients have been perfectly combined and there are no clumps.

Serve with crudités and potato chips.

Alternatively, use the blender or food processor.

SWISS ENCHILADAS

ENCHILADAS SUIZAS

....

Serves 8

Ingredients:
1 chicken breast, cooked and shredded
1 tablespoon of powdered chicken bouillon
12 corn tortillas
1 cup of fresh cream or heavy cream
1 small onion, sliced
1 small onion, whole
1 cup of manchego or Oaxaca cheese, shredded (substitute with Jack or Muenster)
Vegetable oil, as needed
12 tomatillos
1 jalapeño chile, seeded and membrane removed
Salt & pepper to taste

TO PREPARE:

Bring the chicken breast, chicken bouillon and 4 cups of water to a boil in a small saucepan over medium heat until the chicken is tender and fully cooked. Remove the chicken breast from the broth and set aside to cool on a plate. Reserve the broth.

Cook the tomatillos, the whole onion and the chile jalapeño in the reserved broth until the tomatillos and the onion are soft. Transfer the vegetables without the broth to the blender jar and mix until a smooth sauce is achieved.

Heat 2 tablespoons of vegetable oil in a frying pan and add the green sauce. Cook the sauce, stirring occasionally, until it begins to thicken and deepens in color. While the sauce is cooking, taste and adjust the seasoning by adding salt and pepper as needed. Remove from heat and set aside.

Preheat oven to 350°F.

Heat ½ cup of vegetable oil in a small saucepan and when hot, dip the tortillas in it for about 5 seconds on each side. The tortillas should be soft and not crispy. Put them on a plate covered with paper towels to rid them of the excess oil.

Meanwhile, shred the chicken into a small mixing bowl and lightly sprinkle with salt and pepper. Mix around with your hand.

TO ASSEMBLE:

Fill each of the tortillas with a small amount of chicken. Roll them up or just fold them in half and arrange them in an oven safe container or glass Pyrex. Pour the tomatillo sauce evenly over the stuffed tortillas and then drizzle the cream throughout. Arrange the onion slices on top and cover the dish evenly with the shredded cheese. Bake the enchiladas until the cheese melts and the sauce is boiling, for about 30 minutes.

TO SERVE:

Put 3 enchiladas on each plate and serve alongside refried beans.

WHITE FISH BAKED IN SEA SHELLS

CONCHAS DE PESCADO AL HORNO

Serves 8

Ingredients:
8 large flat ceramic shells
4 small red snapper or tilapia filets, cooked and flaked
1 small onion, sliced
4 tablespoons of butter
3 large garlic cloves, minced
$1/4$ cup of parsley, minced
$1/2$ cup of mayonnaise
$1/2$ cup of sour cream
$1/2$ cup of breadcrumbs
6 tablespoons of parmesan cheese, finely grated
4 limes, cut in halves
Salt & pepper to taste

TO PREPARE:

Preheat oven to 350°F.

Rinse and pat dry the raw fish filets. Place them in an oven safe container, lightly sprinkle them with salt and pepper, put one tablespoon of butter on each one and cover them with the sliced onion. Bake for about 15 to 20 minutes until almost done. Remove them from the oven and set aside to cool.

Meanwhile, line a baking sheet with the flat ceramic shells and set aside. Mix half of the parmesan cheese with the breadcrumbs and set aside. Chop the parsley and set aside.

Once the fish has cooled down enough to be handled with the hands, discard the onions and shred it apart directly into a mixing bowl. Add the minced garlic, the minced parsley, mayonnaise and sour cream, and half of the parmesan cheese. Mix well until the ingredients are completely incorporated and adjust the seasoning by adding salt and pepper if needed.

Fill the ceramic shells generously with the fish mixture and sprinkle them with enough bread-crumb and parmesan mix to cover them evenly and lightly. Place the shells in the oven and bake them for about 20 minutes or until the fish turns a golden brown around the edges and they look steamy and hot.

TO SERVE:

Place each shell on an appetizer size plate and put a half lime on every plate. Squeeze the juice of the lime over the fish. This dish is a delicious and satisfying appetizer, but can also be used as a side dish or even as a main dish. Serve alongside saltine crackers.

TIN FOIL BAKED SEA BASS IN A TEQUILA-CHIPOTLE SALSA

FILETE DE RÓBALO EMPAPELADO
EN SALSA DE TEQUILA Y CHIPOTLE

Serves 6

Ingredients:
6 pieces of foil, 8x8 inches each
6 filets of Sea Bass (you can substitute with Sword fish or for a lighter taste Red Snapper)
2 oz of Tequila, separated
2 garlic cloves
1 small red onion, sliced
12 cilantro sprigs
1 cube of chicken bouillon
1 small can of chipotle chiles
1 cup of heavy whipping cream
3 lemons, halved
Salt & pepper to taste

TO PREPARE:

Preheat oven to 350°F.

Rinse the fish filets and pat them dry. Baste them lightly with tequila and sprinkle with salt & pepper. Refrigerate for 15 minutes.

Meanwhile, put the garlic, 2 chipotle chiles from the can + 2 tablespoon of their liquid, chicken bouillon, ½ tablespoon of tequila, and the heavy whipping cream in the blender and mix just until the ingredients are well incorporated. *If you over blend the sauce, it will look clumpy as the whipping cream will begin to turn into butter. If this happens, don't worry it is still good to use.*

Bring the fish filets out of the refrigerator and place each one in the middle of a piece of tin foil with the skin side down. Bring the foil sides slightly upward and cover the filets with the sauce. Put a couple of onion slices and cilantro sprigs over each filet and make a tight pocket with the tin foil to prevent the sauce from spilling out while cooking. Put all the tin foil pockets on a baking sheet and bake for 30 minutes. Check for doneness. The fish will flake easily when probed with the fork. Remove the filets from the oven and let the closed pockets sit for 5 minutes before serving.

TO SERVE:

Place 1 fish filet on each plate and open the tin foil pocket to allow the steam out, but don't remove it. It is usually served with a rice dish on the side and a simple salad.

MEATBALLS STUFFED WITH POTATOES AND CHORIZO

ALBÓNDIGAS RELLENAS DE PAPA Y CHORIZO

Serves 6

Ingredients for the sauce:
6 large ripe tomatoes, cut in four pieces
2 dried guajillo chiles, seeded and membrane removed
5 cilantro sprigs
1 white onion, cut in four pieces
2 garlic cloves
2 packets of powdered chicken bouillon
2 cups of water
3 tablespoons of olive oil

Ingredients for the meat:
1 1/2 lbs of 95% lean ground meat, thawed
2 eggs
1 handful of cilantro, finely chopped
2 oz of Worcestershire sauce
1 tablespoon of powdered mustard
1 teaspoon of curry powder
Salt & pepper to taste

Ingredients for the filling:
4 medium sized potatoes, cooked and peeled
1 chorizo sausage
1 white onion, chopped

PREPARING THE SAUCE:

In a heavy bottom saucepan, heat the olive oil over medium heat.

Put the tomatoes, onion, garlic, cilantro, guajillo chiles, and the cup of water in the blender jar and mix well until a smooth sauce is achieved. If the sauce is too thick, add a little extra water. You may need to work in batches. Transfer the tomato sauce into the saucepan with the hot olive oil. Add the packets of chicken bouillon one at a time to make sure you don't over salt the sauce. Mix, cover it, and reduce the heat to low while you prepare the meat.

PREPARING THE MEAT:

Put all of the meat ingredients in a large bowl, sprinkle lightly with salt & pepper and mix until all of the ingredients are well incorporated. Set aside while you prepare the filling.

PREPARING THE FILLING:

Cook the potatoes by boiling, or using the oven or microwave. Set aside to cool. Once cool enough to handle, peel, mash them and set aside. *Don't salt the potatoes because the chorizo is very salty.* Cook the chorizo and the onion until well done and the chorizo breaks easily into small pieces. Mix the chorizo and onion with the mashed potato and set aside.

Increase the heat of the sauce to medium and stir.

MAKING THE MEATBALLS:

Make a small size ball with the meat and press it between your hands. Once you have it looking like a small and flat meat patty (you don't want it too thin though), grab some potato and chorizo filling and place it in the center of the patty. Cover up the potato-chorizo filling by closing up the meat patty forming a ball again and then add it into the tomato sauce. Repeat the procedure until all meatballs are formed.

Once all of the meatballs are in the sauce, increase the heat to medium-high and bring the sauce to a boil. Once it boils, reduce the heat to medium-low and let simmer, covered, for about 20 minutes, checking the meat constantly for doneness. Occasionally stir very gently to prevent the sauce and the meatballs from sticking to the bottom of the pan and to ensure the meatballs are fully covered with the sauce and cooking evenly. The meatballs will be well done after 30 to 45 minutes of cooking in the tomato sauce. Serve immediately.

TO SERVE:

Transfer the meatballs into a deep serving platter. Serve alongside beans, any rice dish, tortillas, fresh jalapeño chiles, and avocado slices.

GREEN BEAN AND TOMATO SALAD WITH BALSAMIC VINAIGRETTE

ENSALADA DE EJOTES Y JITOMATE CON VINAGRETA DE BALSÁMICO

Serves 6

Ingredients for the Salad:
1 lb of green beans, halved and cooked (boiled)
1 lb of small round red tomatoes, finely chopped and without seeds
1/4 cup of cilantro, finely chopped
Cold water and ice, as needed

Ingredients for the Vinaigrette:
1 cup of extra virgin olive oil
1/2 cup of vinegar
2 spoons of Worcestershire sauce
1 spoonful of granulated chicken bouillon
1 teaspoon of dry oregano
1/2 teaspoon of sugar
1/2 teaspoon of powdered mustard
1/2 teaspoon of powdered curry
2 limes
2 garlic cloves, minced

TO PREPARE THE SALAD:

Slice the green beans in half and cook them in boiling water. When cooked, transfer them into a mixing bowl containing cold water with ice, toss them around for about 1 minute and then drain completely. Set aside.

Chop the cilantro and the tomatoes, and put them in a salad bowl. Add the green beans and toss lightly to incorporate all ingredients. Set aside.

TO PREPARE THE VINAIGRETTE:

Put all of the dressing ingredients in a glass bottle or jar with a lid. Shake the vinaigrette vigorously for about 1 minute. Refrigerate until ready to use.

TO SERVE:

Add 1/2 of the vinaigrette to the salad and toss to mix well. Whatever is left over of the vinaigrette, serve at the table.

GRANDMA FLORA'S CHOCOLATE MOUSSE

MOUSSE DE CHOCOLATE DE LA ABUELA FLORA

Serves 8

Ingredients:

8 oz of dark or semisweet chocolate
$1/2$ cup confectioner sugar
8 eggs, separated
$1/2$ teaspoon of instant coffee, diluted in $1/2$ ounce of water
(you can also substitute with $1/2$ oz of Kahlua or cherry liquor)
$1/8$ teaspoon of cream of tartar

TO PREPARE:

Melt the chocolate over a water bath by placing the chocolate pieces in a small saucepan over a larger one containing boiling water, while stirring gently and ocassionally. *Take care not to allow even a droplet of water to touch the chocolate as this will harden the chocolate and the dessert will not be able to be prepared.*

Whisk or beat the egg yolks until they are light and fluffy. Set aside.

Once the chocolate is smooth and completely melted, remove it from the heat and add it to the previously whisked yolks. Mix them well together with a whisk in a fast motion to prevent the yolks from cooking and then add the confectioner sugar. Lastly, add the diluted coffee, Kahlua or cherry liquor. Set aside.

Beat the egg whites until stiff peaks form. Add the chocolate sauce in a slow, thin stream while enveloping them carefully into the egg whites. *Take care not to rid the egg whites of their air content as this is what gives the mousse its characteristic airy texture.* The motion of gentle enveloping is what will prevent the egg whites from losing their air content.

Pour the mousse into individual glass cups or a large glass bowl and refrigerate until set for about 2 or 3 hours.

HONEY-CINNAMON SWEET POTATOES

CAMOTES CON MIEL Y CANELA

Serves 8

Ingredients:
8 sweet potatoes
4 oranges, squeezed
2 tablespoons of honey
2 teaspoons of cinnamon
1/2 stick of butter, cut into small cubes
Marshmallows, as many as needed

TO PREPARE:

Boil the sweet potatoes until they are very soft to the touch, slightly overcooked. Drain and set them aside to cool and dry. Once the sweet potatoes are cool enough to handle, peel them.

Preheat oven to 325°F.

Squeeze the oranges into a small bowl, add the honey and the cinnamon and whisk well.

Mash the peeled sweet potatoes until very smooth and add the orange juice mixture. Then mix in the butter cubes. Incorporate well and transfer the mashed sweet potatoes to a glass Pyrex or baking pan. Top with as many marshmallows are needed to fully cover the sweet potatoes. Bake until all the marshmallows have melted and their tops are golden to dark brown.

My mother, Sylvia, is a woman of many passions. She is kind natured, selfless and completely devoted to her family and friends. Her attitude has always been that of helping others. After high school, she attended nursing school and after graduating she first worked in the pediatric oncology ward and later on, in the nursery and neonatal units of the American British Cowdray hospital in Mexico City. As time moved forward, she went back to school to study psychology and earned her counselors degree from UCLA in Los Angeles, California.

A few years back during one of my trips to Mexico City to visit her, she showed me one of her diaries and said: "Here, I want you to have this...this is what my life looked liked around the time you were born." For a moment, I doubted that I had heard her correctly, but she waved the small book with a psychedelic pattern in front of me, and continued: "Go on already, take it, I want you to have it." Humbled, I took it.

I read her diary on the airplane back to Buffalo. I was aware that for the most part, she had enjoyed a very pleasant lifestyle, but I never thought I'd be reading -literally- about her golden days. Apparently, the 60's were times of many auspicious events and celebrations in her life, ones she gleefully captured in her daily notes. I could hardly believe I was reading about my own mother.

For the most part, the diary spoke -like any other diary- about her day to day life events, but what was different about it was that she focused so much of her writing on food. She made mention of the foods she enjoyed eating and preparing, the restaurants that she frequented with my father and what they liked to order or what she had eaten for lunch at her parents' home on a particular day. She wrote about innovative cooking techniques, her kitchen experiences and food shopping adventures at *la Merced* and *San Juan* Markets. She even made mention about the foods she prepared for me when I was only a few months old, what I liked and what I disliked. Remarkably, I even came across some loosely attached recipes that she had handwritten on index cards.

As I continued reading, it became clear to me that she had a particular fasci-

nation for the recipes handed down to her by the women she held dear in her life. She even wrote of how privileged she felt to be able to learn about their culinary secrets. It also became evident that the way in which she prepares food even to this day, is greatly biased by the love she feels for the people she is cooking for.

She has mentioned to me on several occasions that the fashion in which she prepares food has been significantly influenced by Nana Pancha, the cook who lived and worked at my grandparents' home since my mother was a very young girl. Nana Pancha worked for my grandparents until old age prevented her from working any more. At that point, everyone chipped in and paid for the rental of an apartment where Nana Pancha and her daughter, Chole, lived until Nana Pancha passed away. After her passing, Chole continued to live in the same apartment and even though her living expenses were taken care of by my family, she additionally supported herself by preparing and selling delicious pickled chiles and vegetables by the jar or the bucket. We named them *Los Chiles de Chole.* My mother helped her sell them to everyone she knew. They were very popular and loved by all who tried them and in no time, she managed to attain quite a large clientele. These days, Chole no longer pickles chiles, for her old age and disabilities keep her from being able to do so, but they are still legendary. Growing up, there was no meal served at my mother's table that wasn't accompanied by the famous *chiles de Chole*...I can still taste them in my memory. My mother used the pickled poblano chiles to prepare cold pickled chiles stuffed with mashed avocado, a dish that is truly sinfully delicious.

While visiting Mexico this last time, I had the chance to once again cook side by side with my mother in her kitchen. As we cooked, she spoke mainly about her past and told goofy stories about the people she loved. I learned that my great-grandfather, Marcos, needed his spoon to be heated up in the oven before eating his soup because he liked it scalding hot; and that my great-grandmother Miriam's favorite dish was *Pescado a la Veracruzana* –Veracruz-style Snapper- but she liked eating it whole, and as she aged, she become prone to swallowing the bones and choking, giving everyone a big scare.

I also had a chance to ask her why she had chosen to share with me the recipes that she did, to which she replied: "It's simple...these are the comfort foods I grew up with...and that you did too." She went on to tell me that she felt it just as important to hand me at least some of my grandmother Hanka's recipes, because no one of my generation or younger has learned how to prepare them and she feared that one day, they'd be forgotten. "By sharing them with you they will not die with me. They will hopefully be enjoyed by others and the generations to come."

PICKLED CHILES POBLANOS AND VEGETABLES

CHILES POBLANOS Y VERDURITAS EN ESCABECHE

Serves 6

Ingredients:

2 glass canning jars, 1 pint capacity each
8 poblano chiles, whole
10 garlic cloves, whole and peeled
20 small cocktail onions or shallots, raw and peeled
2 large carrots, sliced
2 green zucchini, sliced
10 fresh bay leaves
2 sprigs of fresh thyme
2 sprigs of fresh marjoram
4 teaspoons dry oregano
1/2 cup of extra virgin olive oil
1 cup of water
4 cups of white vinegar
1/2 teaspoon of pepper, freshly crackled
4 teaspoons of ground sea salt
2 teaspoons of canning or regular salt

TO PREPARE:

Make a lengthwise slit on each of the chiles and remove the membranes and seeds carefully so as to not break them, and that they can also be used to prepare the avocado stuffed chiles. (recipe found on page 66).

Roast the chiles directly over the open flames of your stove or on a skillet and then peel them completely. Set aside.

Heat the oil in a very large pot or frying pan over medium-high heat. Add the garlic and the carrots, and sauté them for about two minutes. Then add the chiles, onions or shallots, zucchini, and sauté them for 3 more minutes. Now add the bay leaves, oregano, marjoram, thyme, salt, pepper, and stir. Lastly, add the water and the vinegar and bring it to a boil. Once boiling, reduce the heat to medium and allow it to simmer and cook the vegetables, covered, for about 6-7 minutes. Remove from heat and leave it covered and undisturbed for 15 minutes.

Meanwhile, put 1 teaspoon of the canning or regular salt in the bottom of each of the glass jars. Transfer the chiles and the vegetables into the canning jars in equal quantities, cover the jars tightly, shake them softly and stand them upside down, on top of the lid, until they cool. Allow them to marinate for at least 1 day before using although the longer they marinate, the tastier they will be. They last for about 3 to 4 months provided they are kept tightly closed and refrigerated.

TO SERVE:

These pickled chiles can be used for the recipe that follows.

Alternatively, you may wish to use the same recipe using 2 cups of jalapeño chiles instead of the poblanos. These you will be able to use as an accompaniment to several dishes and you don't need to roast or peel them in order to pickle them.

PICKLED POBLANO CHILES STUFFED WITH MASHED AVOCADO

CHILES POBLANOS EN ESCABECHE
RELLENOS DE AGUACATE

Serves 8

Ingredients:
8 pickled poblano chiles and its vegetables to garnish
(refer to recipe found on page 64)
4 large ripe avocados
1/2 cup of cilantro, finely chopped or minced
Salt & pepper to taste

TO PREPARE:

Mash the avocados into a smooth pulp and mix in the minced cilantro. Adjust the seasoning with salt & pepper as needed and set aside.

TO ASSEMBLE:

Arrange the pickled poblano chiles directly on the serving platter and stuff them with the guacamole. Work carefully so as to not break the fragile chiles. Scoop some of the pickled vegetables to decorate the top of the chiles and around the platter.

TO SERVE:

Once the avocado is mashed and stuffed in the chiles, they need to be served immediately so the avocado doesn't brown. These chiles are served at room temperature or chilled, accompanied with tortillas and can be served alongside any meat or rice dish.

BEAN SOUP WITH CACTUS

SOPA DE FRIJOL CON NOPALITOS

Serves 8

1-1 lb package of dried black beans, uncooked
1 cactus paddle
12 cups of water
1 big red ripe tomato, cut in 4 pieces
2 bacon strips, uncooked
1/2 large white onion, cut in 4 pieces
2 cups of milk
2 packets of chicken bouillon
3 tablespoons of olive oil, divided
1 cilantro sprig
2 cups of queso panela or any other fresh cheese that crumbles
Salt & pepper to taste

TO PREPARE:

Rinse the beans under cold water.

In a large and heavy pot put the beans, the 12 cups of water, the onion, the tomato, the 2 uncooked bacon strips, and the cilantro sprig. Cover and bring to a boil over medium-high heat for about 60 minutes. The beans will be done when they are soft to the touch. Check and stir sporadically, making sure that the water doesn't evaporate too quickly. If more water is needed, add some more.

Meanwhile, clean and cut the cactus paddle into ½ inch squares and fry them in a small pan with 1 tablespoon of the olive oil over medium heat. *The cactus paddles are slimy when raw, but when they are cooked they get moist and tender.* Sprinkle them lightly with salt and pepper and set aside.

Crumble or shred the cheese and set aside.

Add the remaining 2 tablespoons of olive oil to a large saucepan and set aside until ready to heat.

When the beans are fully cooked; transfer the beans, the broth and the rest of the ingredients that have cooked with the beans to the blender jar and mix until you get a smooth, thick liquid. You may have to work in batches depending on your blender's capacity. Add the 2 cups of milk to the last batch of beans you mix.

Heat the olive oil you previously added to the saucepan and when hot, start adding the bean soup. When you have all the bean soup in the pot, stir it well. Add the chicken bouillon packets, stir and reduce the heat to medium-low. Allow the soup to simmer for about 10 minutes. Remove it from the heat. Add the cactus cubes at this time, stir and adjust the seasoning with salt and pepper if needed. Serve immediately.

TO SERVE:

This particular soup should be garnished with panela cheese or any other fresh cheese; however, it can also be eaten with shredded Mozzarella or Muenster cheese. Other good toppings are thin fried tortillas strips, sour cream, finely chopped cilantro or parsley and chopped serrano chiles.

MEXICAN STYLE VERMICELLI

FIDEOS AL HORNO

Serves 8

Ingredients:

1 box of spaghetti or vermicelli
6 large red ripe tomatoes or 1 large jar of canned diced tomatoes
1 handful of parsley, coarsely chopped
1 small white onion, cut in 4 pieces
3 garlic cloves
1 chipotle chile (from a can)
3 dry bay leafs
1 tablespoon of dry oregano
2 cubes of chicken bouillon
4 oz of heavy whipping cream
12 oz of manchego, Monterey Jack or Muenster cheese, shredded
Salt & pepper to taste

TO PREPARE:

Boil water in a large pot and add the spaghetti. Cook for 10 minutes, drain and set aside.

Preheat oven to 350°F.

While the pasta is cooking, prepare the sauce. Put the tomatoes, onion, garlic, chipotle chile, parsley, oregano and chicken bouillon in the blender jar and mix very well until a thick sauce is achieved. Taste and adjust the seasoning with salt & pepper if needed.

Quick tip: The sauce is not meant to be runny; it is meant to be a thick, smooth purée. Chop the tomatoes before putting them in the blender to reduce the amount of water that needs to be added to blend. Try blending it without water first and if it doesn't work, add an ounce of water at a time or just enough to release the blades.

Shred the cheese and set aside.

Transfer the pasta into a large mixing bowl and add the sauce. Mix well to fully incorporate the sauce and then transfer it to a large glass Pyrex dish. Drizzle unevenly with the whipping cream and then add the shredded cheese. Bake for about 30 minutes. The cheese on top should be melted and slightly brown around the edges and top. Serve immediately.

SPINACH SALAD WITH PANELA CHEESE AND FRIED TORTILLA STRIPS

ENSALADA DE ESPINACA
CON QUESO PANELA Y TORTILLAS FRITAS

Serves 6

Ingredients for the Salad:
2 bags of baby spinach, washed, completely drained and dry
1 lb of panela cheese finely diced, or fresh cheese or goat cheese, crumbled
4 white corn tortillas, cut in very thin strips
1/2 cup of corn oil, to fry the tortillas

Ingredients for the vinaigrette:
3/4 cup of olive oil
2 large limes
1/4 cup of Worcestershire sauce
1 teaspoon of dry dill
1/2 cup of mayonnaise
1 garlic clove, minced

TO PREPARE:

Cut the tortillas into very thin strips and fry them in the hot corn oil until crispy and golden brown. Set them on a plate covered with paper towels to rid them of the excess oil.

Cut or crumble the cheese to be used and set aside.

Add all of the vinaigrette ingredients to a glass jar with a lid and shake well. Refrigerate until ready to use.

TO SERVE:

Put the baby spinach in a salad bowl, add the chopped or crumbled cheese and top it off with the fried tortilla strips. Don't add the dressing to the salad as it can make it soggy. Allow each person to serve themselves.

CACTUS SALAD
ENSALADA DE NOPALITOS

Serves 6

Ingredients:
5 cactus paddles, uncooked
3 tablespoons of olive oil, separated
1 small white onion, thinly sliced
Maggi sauce (optional)
1/2 teaspoon of dry oregano
1/4 cup of cilantro
6 scallions, without the stem and cut in half
2 tomatoes, chopped with no seeds
3 tablespoons of vinegar
Salt & pepper to taste

TO PREPARE:

Clean and cut the cactus paddles into small strips. Heat 2 tablespoons of the olive oil in a large frying pan over medium-high heat and add the sliced onion, the cactus strips, oregano, and season lightly with Maggi sauce or salt and pepper. *The cactus paddles are slimy when raw, but when they are cooked they get moist and tender.* When the cactus is cooked, remove from heat and set aside to cool.

TO ASSEMBLE:

Once the cactus strips have cooled, transfer them to a mixing bowl and add the remaining tablespoon of olive oil, the vinegar and the chopped cilantro. Toss and mix well to incorporate.

TO SERVE:

Transfer to serving platter and garnish with the chopped tomatoes and halved scallions. Refrigerate the salad until ready to serve.

TORTILLA CASSEROLE

PASTEL AZTECA

Serves 12

```
Ingredients:
24 tortillas
Vegetable oil, as needed
4 lbs of zucchini flower, clean
1 chicken bouillon cube, powdered
6 corn cobs, cleaned and cooked
6 poblano chiles, seeded, membrane removed, roasted, peeled and cut into strips
1 cup of onion, sliced thinly
8 oz of manchego, Muenster or Colby cheese, grated
1 generous cup of sour cream
Salt & pepper to taste
```

TO PREPARE:

Boil the corn until cooked and tender. Once cooked, cut the kernels off the cob.

Meanwhile, rinse the zucchini flower and squeeze out the excess water. Set aside.

Clean the chiles by rinsing them under cold water. Remove the seeds and membranes. Roast, peel and slice the chiles. Set aside until ready to use.

Preheat oven to 400°F.

Heat enough oil in a large frying pan over medium-high heat and fry the onion, zucchini flower, the corn kernels and poblano chile strips, stirring constantly, to prevent sticking and burning. Once the vegetables have cooked down, season them with the chicken bouillon. Remove from heat and set aside.

In a small but deep saucepan, heat approximately 1 cup of vegetable oil over medium heat until very hot. Gently submerge each of the tortillas, one by one, for about 10 seconds each, until they become soft. Put them on a plate covered with paper to towels to rid them of the excess oil.

Cover the bottom of a large glass Pyrex with 8 of the tortillas, overlapping each other. Put ½ of the vegetable mixture on top of the tortillas and add some of the cheese and ⅓ cup of the sour cream.

Cover with another layer of 8 tortillas and then add the last portion of the vegetables. Add some more of the cheese and the other ⅓ cup of the sour cream. Once again, cover the vegetables with the rest of the tortillas and with what is left of the sour cream, spreading it evenly throughout. Finish by sprinkling the rest of the cheese on top.

Bake for 20 minutes.

TO SERVE:

Let the dish sit for 5 minutes outside of the oven before serving. Cut into squares and plate them on individual dishes. This dish can be served as an appetizer, as a side dish to meats or as a vegetarian main dish. It can also be served alongside any style of beans or rice.

Alternatively, you can add cooked shredded chicken breasts and mole sauce (recipe for the mole sauce is found on page 118)

RICE PUDDING

ARROZ CON LECHE

Serves 8

Ingredients:

1 cup of white rice, uncooked
1 can of condensed milk
1 can of evaporated milk
4 vanilla sticks, cut in 4 pieces, alternatively,
use 4 drops of vanilla extract
Water (as needed)
2 cinnamon sticks
3 tablespoons of lemon or orange zest
Raisins (optional)
Powdered cinnamon (optional)

TO PREPARE:

Soak the rice in very hot water for 30 minutes. Drain it, and transfer it to a glass saucepan and completely cover it with hot water again. Add the two cinnamon sticks and the pieces of vanilla sticks and bring it to a boil over medium-high heat, uncovered. Once the water is boiling, reduce the heat to low, stir it gently one last time and cover it with a lid. Allow the rice to cook undisturbed until all the water has absorbed. *Don't stir the rice during the cooking process or it will turn mushy and lose its form.*

The rice will be done when it is soft to the touch, very moist. If the rice is not soft and moist after all of the water has absorbed, add more water and continue with the boiling process until the desired consistency is achieved.

Meanwhile, combine the lime or orange zest with the evaporated and condensed milks in a bowl. Once the rice is cooked to perfection, add the milk mixture and maintain the heat on low. Now mix the rice and milk together gently, so as to not break the rice grains. Cover and let the rice cook for an additional 3 minutes. Remove it from the heat while still covered, and set aside to cool.

TO SERVE:

Transfer the rice pudding to a serving bowl and refrigerate. It can be served hot, at room temperature or cold. Sprinkle with the powdered cinnamon (optional).

ADITIONAL SERVING SUGGESTIONS:

Rice pudding is a well loved Mexican dessert that can be made to have many different flavors and presentations. It can be served in individual cups, garnished with cinnamon sticks and raisins, or with citrus zest or crushed pralines. It can also be served in a big bowl and decorated with fruit wedges and/or flowers.

SYLVIA'S APPLE PIE

PAY DE MANZANA SYLVIA

Serves 6

Ingredients:
6 red apples, unpeeled, diced in small pieces
1/4 cup of brown sugar
Powdered cinnamon, to sprinkle (optional)
2 oz of tequila (optional)
2 cups of all purpose flour
8 oz of butter
2 cup of sugar

TO PREPARE:

Put the unpeeled diced apples in a large mixing bowl and add the brown sugar and tequila, if you are using it. Sprinkle lightly with cinnamon and mix well with your hands. Transfer the apples to a square, medium sized glass Pyrex.

Preheat oven to 350°F .

In another bowl combine the flour, the butter and the sugar with your hands until a uniform, thick dough is achieved. It will be ready when you can form a ball and it stays together.

Pinch a small amount of dough and press it between your hands to flatten it out, and then place it on top of the apples, one piece at a time. Cover the whole pan using this technique. It is important that no openings be left uncovered.

Bake for approximately 30 to 40 minutes. Baking times will vary depending on the type of oven and altitude. The pie will be ready when the dough turns brown around the edges but the rest has a light golden brown hue to it. The dough should also feel like a hard crust.

TO SERVE:

Serve hot or cold with ice-cream on the side, and accompany it with coffee.

It is true to say that my parents, grandparents and the cooks who worked in our family homes were my greatest sources of inspiration; they were my daily teachers so to speak, in my very own cooking school. However, as I've navigated through life, I have bumped paths with many extraordinary people who have had a tremendous impact in my culinary journey; some of them are not even aware of it.

My great-aunt Rebecca, my grandfather Mauricio's sister, used to host the Jewish holiday meals at her home every single year. She would cook and bake for days, not allowing anyone inside her kitchen, and would have a white-gloved waiter serve the meal. I sometimes close my eyes to remember those amazing dinners and find myself thinking about her decadent menu of matzo-ball soup, guefilte fish, Cornish hens, and roast beef... cheesecake, chocolate cake and rugelaj... My thoughts then turn to one of the greatest cooks I know, my aunt Fina, and the outstanding ceviches and desserts she prepares. And I think about my aunt Diana and how she delighted us with her traditional Thanksgiving dinners and Sunday brunches before we moved away; and also about my aunt Nedda, who immigrated to Mexico from her native Cuba and prepared delicious Moros and Cristianos-rice cooked in black bean broth.

My mother calls it a miracle that all three of us, that is me and my two brothers Arturo and Andrés, ended up in the food business. Giving it some thought, it's really no wonder...I mean; after all, we have been surrounded by very talented, food-oriented individuals who influenced us in very positive ways. It is now up to us to carry on with the family traditions that we've been bequeathed and become a source of inspirational guidance to our children, our nieces and nephews, and our future generations.

AUNT FINA'S
TRIO OF CEVICHES

SHRIMP CEVICHE

CEVICHE DE CAMARÓN

Serves 2-4

Ingredients:

1/2 lb of small shrimp, cooked

1 cup of orange juice, freshly squeezed

1/4 cup of lime juice, freshly squeezed

4 tablespoons of red onion or shallots, finely chopped

1/2 cup of tomatoes, finely chopped without skin and seeds

4 tablespoons of cilantro, minced

2 teaspoons of serrano chiles, seeded and sliced

4 teaspoons of olive oil

Salt & pepper to taste

TO PREPARE:

Put all of the ingredients in a mixing bowl and stir to incorporate them well. Allow the ceviche to marinate for at least an hour in the refrigerator before serving. Adjust the seasoning by adding salt and pepper as needed.

TO SERVE:

Serve cold in large wineglasses. Accompany the ceviche with saltine crackers and for an added visual impact, place a thin wedge of lime on the wineglass rim.

RED SNAPPER CEVICHE

CEVICHE DE HUACHINANGO

Serves 2-4

Ingredients:
1/2 lb of Red Snapper or any other white fish cut in small pieces
4 teaspoons of white wine vinegar
1/4 cup of olive oil
2 tablespoons of lime juice, freshly squeezed
4 teaspoons of shallots, finely chopped
4 teaspoons of mint, finely chopped
2 teaspoons of manzano or serrano chiles, finely sliced and without seeds
Pinch of white sugar
1/2 a tomatillo, finely chopped
Salt & pepper to taste

TO PREPARE:

Put all of the ingredients in a mixing bowl and stir to incorporate them well. Allow the ceviche to marinate for at least an hour in the refrigerator before serving. Adjust the seasoning by adding salt and pepper as needed.

TO SERVE:

Serve cold in margarita glasses. Accompany the ceviche with saltine crackers. For an added visual impact, coat the rims of the margarita glasses with sugar or salt.

TUNA FISH OR OCTOPUS CEVICHE

CEVICHE DE ATÚN O PULPO

Serves 2-4

Ingredients:

1/2 lb of octopus, cooked or tuna fish, raw
4 small red onions, sliced thin
4 tablespoons of lime juice, freshly squeezed
4 tablespoons of rice vinegar
4 tablespoons of sesame seed oil
4 tablespoons of peanut oil
2 teaspoons of chile de árbol, finely chopped
1/2 cup of jícama or water chestnuts, finely diced
Black sesame seeds, to garnish
Salt & pepper to taste

TO PREPARE:

Put all of the ingredients in a mixing bowl and stir to incorporate them well. Allow the ceviche to marinate at least an hour in the refrigerator before serving. Adjust the seasoning by adding salt and pepper as needed.

TO SERVE:

Serve cold in martini glasses. Accompany the ceviche with saltine crackers. For an added visual impact, coat the rims of the martini glasses with a mixture of salt and powdered cayenne pepper.

MEXICO CITY MEXICO: THE BEGINNING OF OUR JOURNEY

MEXICO CITY, MEXICO: THE BEGINNING OF OUR JOURNEY

De acuerdo con la leyenda...
"...los Mexicas abandonaron Aztlán en busca de un lugar en el cual construir su imperio. El dios Huitzilopochtli —el más adorado de los dioses- les indicó que el lugar apropiado sería ese en donde vieran a un águila real devorando a una serpiente parada en un nopal. Por 200 años buscaron hasta que al fin encontraron la señal...ahí en un islote en el lago de Texcoco, vieron a un águila real parada en un nopal devorando a una serpiente...Ahí construyeron Tenochtitlán..."

According to legend...
..the Mexicas left Aztlán searching for the land on which to build their empire. God Huitzilopochtli – their most adored deity- had indicated that the accurate location would be where they would witness a bald eagle devouring a snake on top of a cactus plant. For 200 years they searched until they found the signal...in a small islet in the middle of Lake Texcoco was a bald eagle standing on a cactus plant, devouring a snake...there they built Tenochtitlán..."

Mexico City...the once great Tenochtitlán...land of an ancient prophecy and capital city of the Aztec kingdom. Conceptualized and built by a nomadic group of people known as the Mexicas that were led by the belief that they were to establish a great city at the precise location where an eagle devouring a snake atop a cactus plant would be spotted. Such prophecy came to be at the swampy banks of an islet in Lake Texcoco, a most unfavorable location for erecting a city. Nevertheless, the Mexicas rose above all difficulties and not only built a magnificent city, but one of the greatest and most powerful civilizations of that time; it all happened around the year of 1325. The image of the prophetic vision remained so strong throughout the centuries, that it became the coat of arms of Mexico during the establishment of the Mexican Republic. The coat of arms is used as the United Mexican States official seal and it is also the design that embellishes our national flag.

After the Spanish invasion of 1521, the great Tenochtitlán, the swampy city, was eventually conquered; and in just months, much of the city was destroyed. Mexico City today is built on top and around what used to be Tenochtitlán. This is one of the reasons that portions of the historical downtown area are sinking, an example being the magnificent *Palace of the Beautiful Arts*. Archeological expeditions have uncovered remains of the great city, but excavation work done by city workers has also accidentally rendered results. Such is the case of the findings of el *Templo Mayor* -the main temple of Tenochtitlán- while digging a new route for the subway line just a little over 30 years ago.

Mexico...a site of good omen, the land that embraced and welcomed my grandparents and great-grandparents when no other country would; the land that saw the birth of my parents, my siblings and my children; the land where I was raised, the one place I consider my homeland even though I've moved away; the land I so wholeheartedly adore and the geographical location of where our book-writing journey takes place.

Our travel plans were to arrive in Mexico City and stay just for a couple of days. I wanted to visit family and friends, prepare some interviews and go on a day-long expedition to the *San Juan* Market. We were also planning on taking a few staged food photographs at my mother's home before hitting the road. The idea behind the traveling was to visit my favorite locations within the Mexican Republic in hopes of recapturing memories and meeting up with people from my past. For the most part, that's what happened but destiny had already planed to delay us for a couple of days.

The trip had a peculiar start. To begin with, there are no direct flights from Buffalo, NY to Mexico City, so we had to take multiple connecting flights. Our flight from Houston to Mexico City was severely delayed because a bird hit the plane and ended up shredded to pieces in one of the airplane's turbines, completely disabling the aircraft. I do have to say though that we had a fine time while stranded at the Houston airport waiting for the alternate plane to arrive. The highlight had to be forfeiting airplane food and dining instead on popcorn shrimp and crocodile meat.

Upon landing at the Benito Juárez airport in Mexico City, we approached the rent-a-car booth with our reservation documents in hand but because we were so delayed, they had no obligation to honor the reservation. We exhausted all other car-rental options and frustrated and worn out, we took a taxicab to the hotel.

The hotel we stayed at is strategically located right in front of the *Angel of Independence*, a very significant landmark and a popular hang-out place for protestors of any genre, mainly political. It also sits on a street called *el Paseo de la Reforma*, a beautiful informal replica of the illustrious *Avenue des Champs-Élysées* in Paris, which also happens to be one of the city's main arteries. When protestors block this road, the city gets bombarded with an excess of multitudes and traffic, and complete chaos reigns; particularly in the downtown area.

Because we were without a car, my mother agreed to pick us up and take us to the *San Juan* Market. Scott wanted to take pictures, my mother wanted to do some food shopping and I wanted to walk down memory lane with my son Patrick for a while, so it worked well for all. She was, however, incredibly delayed in traffic. Aha!!! The moment we set foot outside the hotel, the culprit of the traffic was instantaneously revealed. Protestors had found their usual clash grounds but this time, things were a tad different; they were taking off their clothes and rallying in the nude. Their tactics worked, for they quickly captured the attention of every single passerby, creating worse traffic and larger crowds than usual, paralyzing the city.

To add to the excitement, world renowned photographer Spencer Tunick was in town. Spencer Tunick is famed for documenting live nude bodies in public places. He takes photographs of hundreds and even thousands of nude people who meet at an appointed place and time, usually set up through his website. That very same day, *El Zócalo de la Ciudad de México –* Mexico City's downtown main plaza- was the chosen location where thousands of people were to gather and pose in the nude for the acclaimed photographer.

To make matters a heck of a lot more interesting, yours truly, the savvy traveler, refused to bring her credit cards along for the trip and had advised Scott to do the same. I mean come on...every time I talk to my mother she complains about crime...why would I bring anything but travelers' checks and prepaid travel money cards? Needless to say, the credit card situation made renting a car the conventional way impossible. But thanks to my friend Fabrizio, who knows the owner of a rent-a-car franchise in Mexico City, we were able to pull some strings and finally rent an auto without the need of plastic. Despite all the chaos though, we managed to move around and get to the places we wanted and needed to be.

THE PYRAMIDS OF TEOTIHUACÁN

THE PYRAMIDS OF TEOTIHUACÁN

for Nedda, my aunt
"azúcar y canela hacen la vida buena" –dicho mexicano

In hindsight, our extended stay in Mexico City proved to be a good thing. With our extra time there, we had a chance to visit the Teotihuacán Pyramids. Although they weren't included in our original itinerary, they always rank high on my list of places to go to when visiting back home. Situated approximately 50 kilometers from Mexico City, it makes it an ideal location to spend the day.

Teotihuacán was a magnificent city, a city of splendor, the greatest and largest of its time. It was home to an extraordinary multiethnic civilization that had, in fact, nothing to do with the Mayas, the Mexicas or the Aztecs. By the time the Mexicas came across Teotihuacán on their way to Lake Texcoco, where they would eventually build Tenochtitlán -the great Aztec kingdom- Teotihuacán had been deserted and in ruins for a very long time, perhaps even for entire centuries.

The Aztecs named the ancient city Teotihuacán. Teotihuacán, in the Náhuatl language means the City of the Gods, or more precisely, the City where the Gods were born. Although most of what we know about Teotihuacán today is based on legend, archeological findings and very few history chronicles, it is believed that the people of Teotihuacán were a civilization of superb warriors who also had an incredible knowledge of agriculture and technical prowess in architecture. To this day, Teotihuacán remains a place of speculation, contradiction and imagination.

I find it amazing that today you can still walk down the *Calzada de los Muertos* -street of the dead- the "main street" of Teotihuacán, in the same fashion as the teotihuacano people did more than 2000 years ago. Upon arriving and passing through the gates, the ruins of this ancient city greet and captivate you with a superb view. Almost immediately, it becomes clear that the most important structures of the city had to be the pyramids that go by the name of the Sun and the Moon. It is startling to see them not only still standing so sturdy, but for the most part, intact. They are not only to be admired; they are also to be experienced. Visitors are allowed to climb up the hundreds of steps to the top of the pyramids and then stay there as for long as they want, enjoying the views.

And then there is the Temple built in honor of god *Quetzalcóatl* and the Palace of the Butterflies and other buildings that although smaller in size, are no less captivating. When I'm there, I try to imagine what this city used to look like during its time of splendor. I visualize an energetic city filled with people dressed in colorful attire going on about their daily business, bartering their wares, washing their clothes, caring for their families; I picture the warriors getting ready to fight and then returning triumphant with their human sacrifices; the market place buzzing with activity

and the temples full of crowds during moments of worship and celebration.

Teotihuacán's supremacy came to an end after a series of unfortunate events, but it didn't happen overnight. The city began to weaken because the people were close to exhausting all of their natural resources, their farmlands dried up, political conflicts arose in their adjacent townships and mayhem reigned throughout; to make matters even worse, they were invaded by the Chichimeca peoples who were looking to fight in order to conquer fertile lands. It is believed though, that it was the teotihuacano people themselves who destroyed and tried to burn their city down before mysteriously abandoning it and vanishing forever.

Pre-Hispanic civilizations based their daily diet on vegetables and certain beans. The most important staples of their diet were corn, beans and chiles. They also successfully cultivated and enjoyed eating avocado, zucchini, pumpkin, tomatoes, cactus plants and *maguey* –a type of cactus- and cacao beans, amongst others.

Corn was such an important component of their daily lives, that it was also an object of veneration. They would treat it with kindness for they feared the wrath of the gods if they didn't. They believed that if corn was somehow wasted, the gods would bring about drought, and with drought would come hunger.

Their meat options were relatively scarce. They raised turkeys and hairless dogs called *xoloitzcuintli* in captivity - yes, dogs to eat - but had to hunt for squirrels, snakes, iguanas, frogs, rats, and deer. And, those civilizations that thrived along river banks or oceans, were also known to have skillful fishing techniques.

Pre-Hispanic civilizations took advantage of what mother earth provided them with, and since they were not picky eaters either, they gathered insects and worms to complement their diets. Crickets, *gusanos de maguey* – maguey cactus worms- *escamoles* and *jumiles* were eaten back then and are still a very popular delicacy in this day and age.

When visiting Teotihuacán, you have to eat at a restaurant called la Gruta. It is a must. The restaurant actually sits inside a natural cave and it's been around since 1928. La Gruta is one of my favorite restaurants. For years now, it's been mostly a tourist destination. They began adding fajitas to their delectable Mexican menu and they hiked their prices making it ridiculously expensive, but the experience of eating there and the service you receive is second to none. The environment is very festive and relaxed; mariachis walk around serenading guests at their table and throughout the day, guests are treated to folkloric ballet shows and regional dance demonstrations.

How else do you end a perfect day at Teotihuacán if not by eating at la Gruta? Everything on the menu is so tempting, that we decided to order various appetizers, desserts and drinks to share.

Appetizers are a big deal in the Mexican food culture. Much like anywhere else in the world they are served an hour or two ahead of a main meal, or at the table while waiting for main dishes to be served. Sometimes, they are even made to replace an entire meal, depending on the occasion.

Mexican appetizers usually consist of *antojitos* and *garnachas*. No precise translation exists for those words, but the first one basically means little cravings or small snacks that can be eaten at anytime of the day, and the latter one refers to foods made by deep-frying maize dough and adding fillings and/or toppings. A good example of these food categories are: *sopecitos*-cooked dough sopes - that are filled with beans and topped with sour cream, minced onion and crumbled cheese; small fried *taquitos* or *quesadillas*; *cazuelitas de queso* –melted cheese- with chiles or mushrooms or chorizo, accompanied with flour tortillas. All of these dishes are served amidst an array of different salsas, fresh cheeses and delicious *guacamoles* with fried tortilla chips or pork rinds. It is also customary to offer alcoholic beverages such as *margaritas* and *micheladas* - a delicious and popular beer drink.

One of my personal favorites in the appetizer category is Guacamole, especially accompanied with fresh, fried corn tortilla triangles also called *totopitos* or with fried pork rinds.

MY FAVORITE GUACAMOLE

MI GUACAMOLE FAVORITO

This recipe serves 8 as an appetizer or 6 if used to accompany a meal.

There is no right or wrong way of preparing guacamole. Much of how it's made is a personal choice. A good thing to consider while planning on making guacamole is how it will be served. Will it be an appetizer, or will it be served alongside a meal? The recipe can be as basic as just mashing the avocado pulp until you get a smooth and uniform paste and then adding a little bit of salt & pepper to taste, or as elaborate as to incorporate liquors or different types of salsas or more traditional ingredients into the dish such as chopped cilantro, tomatoes and green chiles.

In general, good guacamole begins with good avocados. Avocados can be compared to the assorted box of chocolates from the Forest Gump movie; you never know what you're going to get, but I do have some suggestions that might increase the likelihood of choosing really good avocados.

My suggestion is that you buy them before they ripen, that is while they are still as hard as rocks and very green. This way, they can decorate your fruit bowl until they ripen and are ready to be used. To make them ripen faster though, roll them up in a paper bag. This technique works if you are in no immediate hurry to use the avocados, so if you can plan ahead, it is wise to do it this way.

If you can't wait and you need them today, then try this. Take an avocado that looks ripe and grasp it with your whole hand. Gently squeeze it to see if it is soft but still retains its firmness, that avocado will be the one. Never buy an avocado that feels very soft, that looks bruised or that the skin sinks when touched.

Ingredients:
4 ripe avocados
1 small onion, minced
1/2 cup of cilantro, minced
1 small tomato, finely chopped and without seeds
1-2 serrano chiles, very finely chopped, seeds included (optional)
Salt & pepper to taste

TO PREPARE:

Open the avocado by slicing it down the middle, scoop the pulp out with a spoon and discard the pit. Mash the pulp with a fork until a smooth paste is achieved. Add the minced onion, the cilantro, the chiles, and the tomato. Season it with salt and pepper and mix well to combine all of the flavors and the ingredients. Serve immediately.

TO SERVE:

Put the guacamole on a serving platter and surround it with freshly fried homemade tortilla chips, fried pork rinds, crackers or raw vegetables.

Alternatively, if you wish to prepare guacamole using tequila, follow the recipe on page 285.

SOPECITOS

Makes about 15

Ingredients:

2 cups of tortilla dough-mix (MASARICA OR MASECA)
1 1/2 cups of warm water
Vegetable or corn oil, as needed
1 cup of refried beans (page 145)
1 cup of sour cream
1 cup of fresh or feta cheese, crumbled
White onion, finely chopped, as needed
Red or green salsa (page 244-245)

TO PREPARE:

Always make sure to prepare the tortilla dough according to the manufacturer's instructions if available. As a rule of thumb, the basic recipe for the dough is 2 cups of dough-mix, mixed with 1 ½ cups of water. The prepared dough should resemble playdough. If the dough is too watery or sticky, adjust it by adding more dough-mix and if it is too dry, add a little more water.

Combine the water and dough-mix together to prepare the tortilla dough. Once mixed, kneed the dough for a couple of minutes and divide the dough into 10-15 balls, depending on the size you want them to be.

Put one of the dough balls between two plastic bags (sandwich bags) or two pieces of wax paper and set it on the tortilla press. Bring the handle down only halfway; they should resemble thicker disks and not be as flat as tortillas. *Alternatively, if you don't have a tortilla press, press the dough between your hands to form a thick disc without using the plastic bags.* Repeat the process with each of the dough balls and set aside.

Heat a *comal*, a frying pan or a skillet over medium-high heat without oil. Once the *comal* is hot, reduce the heat to medium. Place a couple of the *sopecitos* on top and cook only on one side for 40 to 45 seconds. Remove from the *comal* with a small spatula and using your thumb, press down on the center of the uncooked side of the *sopecito* and immediately return to the *comal*, cooking the indented side for an additional 1 minute. When the dough begins to dry out, again remove it from the comal or skillet and pinch the edges of the indented side between your fingers in an upward fashion to resemble miniature pie crusts. Repeat this process with all of the *sopecitos*. Wrap them in a clean cloth and set them aside until ready to assemble.

TO ASSEMBLE:

Reheat the *comal* or skillet. Using your fingers or a brush, lightly brush the pinched side of the *sopecitos* with the oil and place them on the hot surface with the flat bottom side down. When the oil shows signs of being hot or begins to slightly bubble, remove them from the heat.

TO SERVE:

Fill the *sopecitos* with a small amount of refried beans, salsa, the sour cream, crumbled cheese, and finely chopped onion.

MELTED CHEESE WITH CHILE STRIPS

CAZUELITAS DE QUESO FUNDIDO
CON RAJAS DE CHILE

Serves 4

Ingredients:

1 chile poblano, roasted, peeled and cut into thin long strips
1 cup of Monterrey Jack or manchego cheese, grated
1 tablespoon of butter, plus extra to grease the cazuelita
or flameproof casserole ramekin
8 flour tortillas
Salt & pepper to taste

TO PREPARE:

Fry the roasted chile strips in 1 tablespoon of butter, sprinkle lightly with salt and pepper and set aside.

Lightly grease a *cazuelita* or a small flameproof casserole ramekin. Put the grated cheese in the *cazuelita* and place the chile strips on top of it. Cover with tin foil and put the casserole ramekin on the stove over low heat until the cheese begins to melt, for about 3 minutes. Uncover to continue melting for an additional 1 to 2 minutes or until the cheese is fully melted and slightly bubbling.

*Alternatively, you can melt the cheese in small ceramic ramekins by baking them in a preheated oven until the cheese begins to bubble and is fully melted

TO SERVE:

Serve immediately alongside warm and soft heated flour tortillas and various salsa selections.

*Alternatively, you can prepare the cazuelitas with mushrooms, chorizo and chopped zucchini flowers.

CLASSIC SHAKEN MARGARITAS

MARGARITAS CLÁSICAS

Serves 2

Ingredients:
1/2 cup of premium tequila
1/4 cup of triple sec or other fruity liquor
1 lime, cut crosswise into 5 slices
Coarse sea salt, as needed
1 cup of ice-cubes
2 tablespoons of lime juice, freshly squeezed

TO PREPARE:

Moisten the margarita glass rims with a piece of lime and dip them into the coarse salt to coat the rims lightly.

Combine the ice-cubes, tequila, triple sec, and lime juice in a cocktail shaker. Shake vigorously until the outside of the shaker becomes frosty. Pour the margarita into the prepared glasses and garnish the rims with the lime slices.

MICHELADA

Serves 1

Ingredients:
1 light beer
1 large lime, freshly squeezed
1 thick lime wedge
Maggi sauce, as needed
Worcestershire sauce, as needed
Tabasco sauce, as needed
Sea salt & pepper, freshly ground
Ice

TO PREPARE:

Moisten the rim of a beer glass with lime and dip it into the salt to coat it generously. Pour the lime juice, the Maggi, Tabasco and Worcestershire sauces, and some freshly ground pepper into the beer glass. Mix well. Tilt the glass sideways and pour the beer slowly so as to not make much foam. Garnish with a lime wedge if desired.

CORN CAKE WITH STRAWBERRY SYRUP

PASTEL DE ELOTE CON JARABE DE FRESAS

Ingredients:
3/4 cup of brown sugar
1 1/4 cup of white sugar
1/4 lb of butter + extra for greasing the cake pan
5 eggs
1/2 teaspoon salt
2 cups of flour
1 tablespoon of vanilla extract
1 1/2 cup of heavy whipping cream
2 cups of corn kernels, fresh or frozen (thawed to room temperature)
2 teaspoons of baking powder

Strawberry Syrup:
1 package of (fresh or frozen) strawberries (about 2 cups)
1/2 cup of superfine white sugar

TO PREPARE:

Preheat oven to 350°F.

Mix the butter and sugar with a hand-held mixer until light and fluffy.

Add the eggs one at a time until each one is perfectly incorporated before adding another one.

Add the flour and the heavy whipping cream a little at a time by alternating. Add the baking powder, the salt and the vanilla extract. Keep beating until well incorporated.

Fold in the corn kernels and transfer the batter into a heavily buttered 10-inch round cake pan or a Bundt cake-mold. Bake the cake for approximately 65 minutes or until cooked. The cake will be done when you insert a toothpick down the center and it comes out moist but clean.

TO MAKE THE STRAWBERRY SYRUP:

While the cake is baking, blend the strawberries until they liquefy. Transfer to a small saucepan over medium-low heat. Add the superfine white sugar and mix well to dissolve. Reduce the heat to low and stir constantly. Once the syrup begins to thicken, transfer it to the serving container. Serve warm on the side or on top of the corn cake.

MILK CARAMEL CRÊPES WITH CHOPPED PECANS AND MANGOES FLAMBÉ

CREPAS DE CAJETA CON NUECES PICADAS Y MANGOS FLAMEADOS

Makes 15-20 crêpes

Ingredients for the Crêpes:
2 1/2 cups of whole milk
5 large eggs
1 cup all purpose flour
6 tablespoons butter, melted, cooled slightly
2 tablespoons of sugar
3/4 teaspoon of salt
Zest of 1 bitter orange
* Some additional butter will be needed for buttering the frying pan.

Ingredients for the milk caramel sauce:
1 cup of cajeta (milk caramel, recipe found on page 208)
2 tablespoons of butter
1/2 cup of orange juice
2 tablespoons of rum

Ingredients for the mangoes flambé:
16 oz of mangoes, fresh or canned, cut into large pieces
2 tablespoons of butter
2 tablespoons of dark brown sugar
2 tablespoons of tequila

TO GARNISH:
1/2 cup of pecans, chopped (optional)

TO PREPARE THE CRÊPES:

Combine the whole milk, eggs, flour, melted butter, sugar, salt, and the orange zest in a mixing bowl using a whisk or a hand-held mixer. Let stand 1 hour at room temperature and whisk again before making the crêpes. Brush a small non-stick frying pan lightly with melted butter and heat it over medium-high heat. Pour a scant ¼ cup of batter into the frying pan and grabbing it by the handle, remove it from the stove and make circular motions to fully coat the bottom of the pan, as if making a thin, round pancake. Reduce the heat to medium-low and cook the crêpe until it is slightly golden around the edges, for about 1 minute. Using a small spatula, turn the crêpe over and cook for an additional 10 seconds. Transfer to a plate covered with paper towels. Set them aside while you prepare the milk caramel sauce.

TO PREPARE THE MILK CARAMEL SAUCE:

Melt the butter over medium-low heat and add the milk caramel –*cajeta*- and orange juice. Stir for about 5 minutes to combine well. Add the rum, flame it and let it burn off.

TO PREPARE THE MANGOES FLAMBÉ:

Melt the butter in a frying pan over medium heat and add the mangoes. Stir them around to coat them with the butter and fry them lightly. Add the brown sugar and stir to incorporate well. Add the tequila, flame it and let it burn off.

TO ASSEMBLE:

Fold the crêpes in half and then half again to form a triangle, place them on a serving platter or individual plates, drizzle the hot milk caramel sauce over the crêpes and sprinkle them with the chopped pecans. Put a few flamed mango pieces over the crêpes and serve immediately.

Alternatively, if cajeta is not available to you and you don't have time to prepare it, follow the same recipe using Dulce de Leche, which is easily accessible in supermarkets everywhere. The taste will vary and the consistency of the sauce will be different but they will turn out delicious just the same.

THE DAY OF THE DEAD AND THE DAY OF ALL SAINTS

THE DAY OF THE DEAD
AND THE DAY OF ALL SAINTS

in memory of Alejandro, my father
in memory of Enrique, my uncle
"llévate mi alma, quítame la vida, pero de mi pan de muerto ni una mordida"
–dicho mexicano

Mexico is characterized as a country with folklore and traditions that have been handed down from generation to generation. One of the most important celebrations countrywide is the Day of the Dead and the Day of All Saints. It is celebrated by everyone regardless of race or ethnicity, as it is not only a grand celebration of life itself, but it also coincides with the end of harvest; therefore, it is also a celebration of abundance.

The Day of the Dead is one of my favorite holidays. When I lived in Mexico City, I would either spend the celebrations in a small town known as San Andrés Mixquic- a short drive away from the city - or I would venture even farther to the island of Janitzio, in the state of Michoacán. Both places are huge attractions and become packed with visitors.

People go to these charming places with the objective of walking through the cemeteries to look at the tombstones and their abundant ornaments. Quesadillas, tacos, tamales, alcoholic beverages, and other goodies are sold throughout the night while people pray, sing and celebrate to the tune of mariachis or other musical groups. It is a spectacle never to be forgotten and a testament of the how strong the cult of death still remains.

Pre-Hispanic Mexico considered life to be unstable and transitory and so they thought that humankind was responsible for the sustenance of the cosmos and an intermediary between the heavens and the earth. They believed that their mission was to perpetuate creation, and that creation provided the Universe with the needed energy to keep on going. It was also thought that it was possible to perpetuate creation by performing sacrificial practices such as penitence and ritual body tortures. Death offerings allowed for the possibility of liberating this vital energy back into the universe. Therefore, according to this point of view, death was considered to be a resource of life.

During these sacrificial celebrations, people danced and chanted. Offerings were made to the gods as well as the deceased by building magnificent altars that were decorated with ornaments such as flowers, corn, hens, and incense. These were also the locations where young girls and slaves were ultimately sacrificed as human tributes to the gods.

When the Spanish invaders arrived to the new world, they brought with them a new faith and with that came the destruction of this ancient civilization. They justified this as a Christian mission and forced everyone to adapt to their faith and set of beliefs, in consequence, significantly eroding the natives' pagan ways.

Happily, not everything was eradicated. Consider the cult of death. What really ended up happening was a fusion of the ideas that both cultures had. The strength of the new church altered the way that death was perceived, but the pre-Christian ways weren't totally eliminated. The cult of the dead continued and so instead of fighting it, the Spanish made the pagan practices coincide with the Catholic ways of honoring the dead. On the Day of All Saints, November 1st, offerings were made to the young children who had passed away; the next day, November 2nd, offerings were made to the adults. This day came to be known as the Day of the Dead.

Pre-Hispanic culinary practices were not eradicated either. Spanish influences did not replace this ancient gastronomy, it only enhanced it. The result of this cultural diffusion proved to be a very rich interchange of foods, spices and cooking techniques that established the foundations of what Mexican cuisine is today.

To this day, we still construct altars of every shape and size to honor those who have passed before us. We decorate them with *cempazúchitl* flowers –marigolds- bread of the dead, hot chocolate, *atole*, *mole*, alcoholic beverages, water, fruits, candy, salt, incense, photographs, and if the altar is dedicated to a young child, with toys.

When setting an altar, we take great care to incorporate the foods and artifacts that the person enjoyed while alive. It is believed that the spirit of the deceased comes down from the heavens on this day and refuels by inhaling the essence of his or her favorite foods. We also embellish the altars with satin or silk fabrics and *papel picado* –a traditional and colorful Mexican paper decoration.

In addition to the preferences of our long gone loved ones, there are some elements that always need to be present in an altar, as they are essential to receiving the souls of the dearly departed.

Each one of the altar elements is characterized by certain mysticisms. Water is considered to be a source of life and it is offered to visiting souls to quench their thirst after such a long journey and to sustain them on their way back. It also represents the purity of the soul. Salt, which is another one of the elements that is a must in every altar, is believed to aid the body against putrefac-

tion. Flowers are displayed as a symbol of joy and celebration that also aromatize the environment while the soul of our beloved is present.

Lit candles and waxes are meant to guide and orient the souls, but they also represent the light, faith and hope. In some communities, each candle represents a dead relative. This means that the number of candles that are placed on the altar will depend on the total number of souls that the family is expecting to return. Incense and/or *copal* – a fossilized resin that burns and produces an odor much like incense- are thought to be the elements that elevate prayer to the heavens. They are also used to cleanse spaces of evil spirits, allowing the soul a smooth descent into its previous home without facing any dangers.

Alcoholic beverages are offered with the intention to lure the souls into visiting and to intoxicate them with happy memories from the past.

And then, of course, there is the food to be displayed: the bread of the dead; *calaveritas de azúcar o chocolate* – sugar or chocolate skulls- or other types of *alfeñiques*: sugar based figurines which are decorated with colorful icing; quesadillas filled with cheese, zucchini flowers, mushrooms or *rajas con crema; mole* with chicken or turkey, candied pumpkin, savory and sweet *tamales* and *atole*, Mexican hot chocolate and *churros* – fried dough.

PAN DE MUERTO: BREAD OF THE DEAD

The Bread of the Dead has its origins in central Mexico, but it has been greatly embraced all across the Mexican Republic. Bakeries only prepare them during this time of the year in honor of the deceased. This type of bread holds a very special place in altars and it is the second most traditional piece of bread in the country, only to be outnumbered by the *Rosca de Reyes* -kings cake- during the Christmas celebrations. It is consumed as part of the dessert and accompanied with coffee, milk, Mexican hot chocolate, or atole.

The shape of these breads is round. This most likely depicts the shape of ancient tomb stones; the top middle part represents the base of the skull and the lateral adornments symbolize the bones of the extremities.

The bread is characterized by a spongy consistency, a unique flavor and a light sweetness. It is easy and fun to make and also affordable because most of the ingredients are staple items to every kitchen: flour, yeast, eggs, butter, water, and a touch of orange. It has no filling and given enough time to rise, ensures its spongy consistency.

BREAD OF THE DEAD
PAN DE MUERTO

Ingredients:
5 cups of flour
8 tablespoons of dry active yeast
1/2 cup of lukewarm water
5 eggs plus 5 yolks
5 cups of flour
1/2 lb of butter or margarine, softened
1 cup of white sugar
3 tablespoons of orange juice or water
1 tablespoon of orange zest
1/8 teaspoon of salt
2 eggs, to brush the breads
Superfine white or colored sugar, to sprinkle on top of the breads
Vegetable or corn oil, enough to grease the baking sheets

TO PREPARE:

In a mixing bowl, break up and sprinkle 4 tablespoons of yeast in ½ a cup of lukewarm water. Add ½ a cup of flour; form into a small, soft ball and allow it to rest and rise in a warm spot of your kitchen until it doubles in size, for approximately 15 to 20 minutes.

Sift the rest of the flour with the salt and sugar into a bowl. If you have an electric mixer, attach the bread hook to it and one by one add the 5 whole eggs, the 5 yolks, and then slowly add the softened butter, orange zest, and orange juice or water, and combine the ingredients well at medium speed.

Alternatively: If you don't have an electric mixer, sift the flour, salt and sugar directly onto a counter-top forming a small mountain and press your fist down firmly at the top to make a big enough dent that can hold the eggs, yolks, softened butter, orange zest, orange juice or water. Mix all of the ingredients and knead well.

Incorporate the small dough ball into the prepared dough and knead some more. If you are using the electric mixer, continue to use the bread hook. Don't over knead or mix. Cover the dough with a dishtowel and allow it to rest in a warm spot of your kitchen for 1 hour.

After one hour, preheat oven to 350°F.

Knead the dough only by hand one more time and form the balls for the breads to the desired size. *Keep in mind that they do expand in the oven*. Reserve some of the dough to craft the decorations. Place the balls of dough on a well greased baking sheet, making sure there is enough room for them to raise and expand. Gently press them down to flatten them a little and give the final shape to the bread.

Beat the 2 remaining eggs and brush the breads lightly with it. Decorate the top of the breads by forming tear shaped pieces with the remaining dough and placing them on top of the breads. Again, brush them lightly with the egg. Lastly, sprinkle the breads generously with sugar making sure the whole top and sides of the bread are completely covered. Bake for 40 to 50 minutes or until the top and sides of the breads start taking on a light brown hue. Allow the breads to cool at room temperature. They keep better and last longer if stored in an airtight container. Don't refrigerate.

ALFEÑIQUES: SUGAR FIGURINES

Alfeñique means: cooked sugar paste. It is also referred to as *charamusca* or sugar ribbon. *Alfeñiques* are the traditional sugar figurines confectioned during the Day of the Dead celebrations. Every state has its favorite type of figurines. For instance, in Mexico City, sugar and chocolate skulls are very popular. A very cool detail is that the names of either the departed or those of living relatives are usually written on the skulls' forehead, drawn on to it with a colorful sugar icing. In the state of Puebla, coffins, graves and skulls are also crafted, but these figurines mostly resemble marzipan as they are made with almonds, peanuts and eggs. In the state of Oaxaca the *alfeñiques* are shaped to resemble animals, fruits, crosses, crowns, corpses, and skulls. These particular ones are made with crystallized sugar and filled with honey.

These types of sugar figurines are only available for purchase during the months of October and November. This provides a true spectacle in markets and other locations where they are sold. In essence, they are quite simple to make if you enjoy handcrafting. The perk to making them yourself is that you are not restricted to enjoying them only during the Day of the Dead and the Day of All Saints celebrations.

There are a few different ways to make *alfeñiques*. Some of them are entirely handcrafted and others are made with special tools and molds. I am sharing a recipe that makes beautiful sugar skulls using molds and another one that requires no molds; allowing your creativity to shine through by sculpting and designing your own. Both techniques are great arts & crafts projects for children; my children and I used to have a lot of fun making them together.

To prepare the *alfeñiques* using the following recipe, you don't need any special tools or molds. Just make sure that you do have a large mixing bowl, small paint brushes such as stencil brushes and a sifter, available to use.

ALFEÑIQUES
(NO MOLD REQUIRED)

Ingredients:
Food coloring, different colors
2 cups of powdered sugar
1/3 cup of corn starch
1/2 tablespoon of vanilla
1 tablespoon of corn syrup
1 egg white

TO PREPARE:

Mix the corn syrup, vanilla and egg white in a bowl with your hands. Sift the sugar directly on top of this mixture and keep mixing until all of the ingredients are well incorporated and you can form a ball.

Sprinkle the corn starch over a clean and smooth surface and extend the sugar paste with a rolling pin until it becomes soft and workable (the consistency should be somewhat like playdough). Make small figurines such as crosses, skulls, coffins, fruits, animals, baskets or corpses. As you craft the figurines, set them to dry over a cookie rack for approximately 4 hours. Once they are dry and they can be picked up without breaking or bending, use the small paint brushes to decorate them using the food coloring.

They keep well for about a month in paper or plastic bags. Don't refrigerate.

ALFEÑIQUES
(MOLD REQUIRED)

To prepare the *alfeñiques* using the following recipe, you will need skull molds. They are available in craft and online stores.

```
Ingredients:
Sugar skull molds
1 1/2 lbs of white sugar
1/2 teaspoon of cream of tartar
1 cup of water


Ingredients to decorate:
2 egg whites
Powdered sugar, as needed
10 drops of lime, freshly squeezed
Food coloring
Tin foil of different colors
Wax paper, to make icing tips
```

TO PREPARE:

In a saucepan, dissolve the sugar in the water over medium heat. Bring to a soft boil and reduce the heat to low. Allow the liquid to boil softly for about 12 minutes, mixing from time to time to prevent burning or sticking. Remove from heat, and with a hand-held mixer beat the mixture until it turns opaque white.

Bring the molds together with rubber bands and fill them up. Allow them to dry upside down or according to the molds manufacturer's instructions.

Let them dry at room temperature until the sugar sets. One by one, take the molds and submerge them in water and then immediately take them out. Take the rubber band off and remove the mold. Let them drain and finish drying on a baking sheet or cookie rack.

While the skulls are drying, prepare the icing and decoration items.

With a handheld mixer, beat the egg whites and the lime drops with just enough powdered sugar to form a soft paste; the consistency should resemble cake icing. Divide this paste in 4 or 5 small containers or ramekins and add a few drops of different food coloring to each.

If you have icing tips, use the smallest size. If you don't have icing tips, make them with wax paper by rolling it at an angle tightly at the tip and loose enough on the top to be able to fill it with the icing. Make as many icing tips as you need, one for each color. Cut the tip a little to allow a small flow of icing to come out of it.

TO DECORATE:

Put a small dot of icing behind the tin foil and glue it onto the forehead of the skull. Using the icing tip, decorate around the edges of the tin foil to make it hold and then write the name or the initials of a loved one. Then, decorate the eyes, the head and other areas. The mold kit will most likely give decoration ideas, but there is nothing better than coming up with your own.

REAL QUESADILLAS

QUESADILLAS

Makes about 18 quesadillas

Ingredients for the masa (dough):
2 cups of tortilla dough-mix (MASARICA or MASECA)
1 1/2 cups of hot water
Vegetable oil, to fry
Red Salsa (garnish)
Green Salsa (garnish)
Sour cream (garnish)

Filling options:
Grated cheese
Mushrooms
Zucchini Flower
Rajas con crema (recipe found on page 230)
Any filling of your choice

TO PREPARE:

Always make sure to prepare the tortilla dough according to the manufacturer's instructions if available. As a rule of thumb, 2 cups of dough-mix with 1 ½ cups of water is the general recipe. The prepared dough should resemble playdough. If the dough is too watery or sticky, adjust it by adding more dough-mix and if it is too dry, add a little more water.

Combine the water and the dough-mix to prepare the tortilla dough. Form it into a big ball. From that ball, pinch enough dough to make another 1 ½ inch ball. Place the smaller ball between two small plastic bags or parchment paper and place it in the middle of the tortilla press, and press down hard. *If you don't have a tortilla press, place the tortilla dough between the plastic or parchment paper and use a rolling pin to thin it out. Make sure you get somewhat of a circle. Peel the plastic or parchment paper off before adding the filling(s). You can also make the tortillas by flattening the tortilla dough between the palms of your hands.*

Heat a good amount of vegetable oil in a large and heavy frying pan over medium heat.

Put about 2 tablespoons of grated cheese or any other filling down the middle of the already formed tortillas. Fold over once to cover the filling and close it up by pressing the ends together with your fingers. Transfer the quesadillas gently into the hot oil and fry them for approximately 45 seconds on one side, flip them over and fry for 1 additional minute. Then flip them over again and fry for 15 more seconds. The dough should cook to a beautiful light golden brown.

Always make sure that the oil is hot before putting the quesadillas in it. Otherwise, the dough will absorb too much of the oil and they will become soggy.

Stack the fried quesadillas on a plate covered with paper towels to rid them of the excess oil. Arrange them in a serving platter and serve immediately.

Serve alongside a variety of homemade red or green salsas, guacamole and sour cream.

BLACK MOLE POBLANO WITH CHICKEN OR TURKEY

MOLE POBLANO CON POLLO O GUAJOLOTE

Serves 8

Mole is one of the dishes that better represents Mexican cuisine and it is a personal favorite of mine. *Mole* is a laborious dish that dates back to pre-Hispanic times but, legend tells that it was perfected in convent kitchens in the state of Puebla during colonial times, when the neo-Hispanic cuisines were enriched with European and Asian elements. *Mole* is popularly served during big festivities and celebrations.

Ingredients for the chicken or turkey stock:
16 cups of water (1 gallon)
16 pieces of chicken (breasts, thighs, legs, etc.) or 12 pieces of turkey
2 celery stalks, cut in large pieces
1 medium onion cut in 4 pieces
1 garlic clove, peeled and halved
2 chicken bouillon cubes
Salt & pepper as needed

Ingredients for the mole sauce:
1/2 cup + 2 tablespoons of vegetable or corn oil
7 1/2 oz of ancho chiles, seeded and membrane removed
3 1/2 oz of pasilla chiles, seeded and membrane removed
12 oz of mulato chiles, seeded and membrane removed
4 chipotle chiles
1 1/2 lbs of red tomatoes
1 onion, chopped
10 garlic cloves
5 oz of almonds, peeled
4 oz of peanuts, peeled
8 aromatic cloves, whole
4 grains of black peppercorns
1 cinnamon stick
1/2 teaspoon anise seeds
3 1/2 oz raisins
4 oz of unsweetened powdered confectionery cacao (bitter chocolate)
1 tablespoon of white sugar
1/4 cup sesame seeds
Salt & pepper to taste

TO PREPARE THE STOCK:

Put the water in a large stockpot and bring it to a boil over high heat. Once the water is boiling add the turkey or chicken pieces, the onion, the garlic, and the celery. Cover the stockpot and reduce the heat to medium. Half-way through the cooking process, add the chicken bouillon and allow the liquid to keep boiling until the chicken or turkey pieces are fully cooked, for about 1 hour. Taste the broth and adjust the seasoning by adding salt & pepper if needed. Drain the meat pieces reserving the stock in a different container. Keep the stock and the chicken or turkey pieces separately. *You can make the stock a day or two ahead.*

TO PREPARE THE MOLE SAUCE:

Heat 2 tablespoons of the oil in a frying pan or deep skillet and sauté the ancho, pasilla and mulato chiles for about three minutes. (Reserve the oil in the frying pan or skillet for later use).

Transfer the sautéed chiles into a small bowl with hot water and set them aside to soften for about 30 minutes.

Drain and grind the chiles in a *molcajete*, a *metate* or the food processor until pasty and set aside.

Roast the chipotle chiles and the tomatoes on a *comal* or a skillet. Then peel the tomatoes and purée them with the chipotle chiles in the blender and set aside.

In the same oil and frying pan you used to fry the chiles, sauté the garlic and the onion until translucent, remove them from the oil and blend them to obtain a soft purée. Using the same oil and frying pan, sauté the almonds for five minutes and then add the peanuts, cloves, peppercorns, cinnamon stick, and anise seeds and sauté for an additional 4 minutes. Grind all of these ingredients along with the raisins in the food processor until you obtain a thick paste.

Ideally, use a large clay pot or casserole, but if you don't have one, use a regular casserole or pot. Heat the ½ cup of oil over medium-high heat. Once the oil is hot but not scorching, add all of the ground and puréed ingredients and cook them together for 5 minutes, stirring constantly. Reduce the heat to medium and mix in the powdered cacao and sugar. Continue to stir constantly until all of the ingredients are well incorporated. When the mixture begins to boil, add 4 cups of the reserved chicken/turkey stock you previously prepared; mix well, and reduce the heat to low. Cover the casserole and cook the mole sauce for another 20 minutes. Taste and season with salt and pepper as needed.

Mole should be somewhat of a thick sauce, but if you consider the mixture to be excessively thick, add more broth a little at a time to achieve the desired consistency.

recipe continues on next page...

Add the pieces of chicken or turkey to the casserole containing the mole; fully coat them with the mole sauce and continue to heat for an additional 10 to 15 minutes.

TO SERVE:

You can serve the mole directly from the casserole and allow each person to serve him or herself but you can also plate them individually. Finish off the dish by sprinkling sesame seeds on top.

Rice dishes, tortillas and beans are great accompaniments to this classic dish.

Alternatively, you can now buy pre-made mole paste in almost every large supermarket around the world, so if you don't have the time to prepare mole from scratch, follow this recipe instead:

INGREDIENTS FOR MOLE SAUCE:

2 jars of Doña María or any other mole paste brand
7 to 9 cups of chicken or turkey stock (you might need more depending on desired consistency of the mole) (chicken stock recipe found on page 118-119)
Sesame seeds
Salt & pepper to taste

TO PREPARE THE MOLE SAUCE:

Empty the contents of Doña María mole paste into a large stockpot or clay casserole. Add 7 cups of the chicken or turkey broth and over medium heat, stir until well incorporated with a wooden spatula. Keep adding more chicken stock until the mixture is no longer lumpy but is still somewhat thick and completely smooth. When adding more stock, make sure you only add ½ cup at a time, taking your time to incorporate it well. Mole is a salsa, a bit thicker than regular plain salsa, but it must be smooth. Check for flavor and if needed, add salt and pepper to adjust the seasoning.

Add the pieces of chicken or turkey to the casserole containing the mole and heat them for about 10 to 15 minutes, the pieces need to be fully coated with the mole sauce.

CANDIED PUMPKIN

CALABAZA EN TACHA

Ingredients:

3 lbs of pumpkin or acorn squash, with skin, cut in uneven chunks

5 cinnamon sticks

2 tablespoons of vanilla extract

The zest of 1 lemon

The zest of 2 oranges

The juice of 2 oranges

1 1/2 cups of dark brown sugar

3 cups of water

Accompaniment suggestions:

Sour cream and/or evaporated milk

TO PREPARE:

Wash and clean the pumpkin shell, remove all the seeds and fiber strands, and cut into uneven chunks. Set aside.

Put the water, orange juice, orange zest, lemon zest, vanilla, and dark brown sugar in a large heavy saucepan over medium heat and mix well. Add the pumpkin chunks and the cinnamon sticks. Stir well to ensure you coat all the pumpkin pieces well with the syrup and cover the saucepan with a lid. As soon as this light syrup begins to boil, uncover, stir the pumpkin one more time, reduce the heat to medium-low, and cover again until all of the liquid has evaporated and the pumpkin is fully cooked and glazed. Gently mix from time to time during the cooking process to ensure full coating and prevent sticking and burning.

Remove from heat and allow it to cool. It is best when served at room temperature.

SERVING SUGGESTIONS:

You can eat it as is or accompanied with a dollop of sour cream or with a drizzle of evaporated milk.

CHURROS

Makes about 15-20

Ingredients:
1 1/2 cups of self-rising flour
6 tablespoons of light brown sugar
2 large eggs + 1 egg yolk
2 1/2 tablespoons of water
1 tablespoon of lemon or orange zest
1/2 teaspoon of cinnamon, ground
1 teaspoon of vanilla extract, preferably Mexican
1 cup of superfine white sugar, for dusting
Corn or vegetable oil, enough to fry

TO PREPARE THE CHURROS:

You don't need any special equipment to make this recipe. If you have a churro maker all the better, but if you don't, all you need is a pastry bag with a 3/8-inch star tip.

In a stainless steel bowl, whisk or beat the light brown sugar, eggs, egg yolk, water, lemon or orange zest, powdered cinnamon, and vanilla extract and set aside. Let rest for about 5 minutes and then stir in the flour.

Heat enough of the corn or vegetable oil -about 1 ½ inch deep- in a large saucepan over medium-high heat. The optimal temperature should be 355°F. *Please note that if the oil is not completely heated to the right temperature, the churros will become soggy.*

While the oil is heating, pour the superfine white sugar in a medium sized bowl and set it aside until you are ready to dust the churros.

Spoon the dough into the pastry bag fitted with the star tip. Squeeze about 4 inches of dough through the pastry bag and cut it with a pair of scissors while almost touching the uncooked churro with the oil and then allowing it to drop. This procedure also allows the churro to maintain its shape. Work gently and skillfully to avoid being splattered by the hot oil.

Working in batches, deep-fry the churros until they develop a golden brown throughout turning them occasionally, for about 1 to 1 ½ minutes on each side. Transfer the fried churros to a plate covered with paper towels to rid them of the excess oil.

Add a few churros at a time to the bowl containing the sugar and toss the churros around to fully coat them.

TO SERVE:

Eat them alone or accompany them with a mug of Mexican hot chocolate, *atole* or coffee.

MEXICAN STYLE HOT CHOCOLATE

CHOCOLATE CALIENTE

Serves 4

Ingredients:

3 cups of water

6 oz Mexican chocolate such as Abuelita or Cortéz
(they come in 3.1 oz disks, so use 2)

2 oz of heavy whipping cream

Powdered cayenne pepper (optional)

TO PREPARE:

Put the water and the chocolate in a medium sized saucepan and bring it to a simmer over medium heat. Stir constantly and gently until the chocolate tablets dissolve completely.

Remove the dissolved chocolate from the heat and transfer it into the blender. Mix on high until completely smooth and frothy. Add the heavy whipping cream and blend some more. Serve the hot chocolate in mugs and lightly sprinkle them with the powdered cayenne pepper if desired.

GUAVA MAIZE DRINK

ATOLE DE GUAYABA

Makes 4 cups

Ingredients:
3/4 cup of canned or fresh guava, coarsely chopped
2 1/2 cups of water
12 oz of evaporated milk
1 1/2 tablespoons of corn starch
2 tablespoons of cold water, to dilute the corn starch
3 tablespoons of dark brown sugar

TO PREPARE:

Add the measured guava pieces and the 2 ½ cups of water to a medium size saucepan. Bring the water to a boil over medium-low heat and as soon as it begins to boil, reduce the heat to low, and let it simmer for 10 minutes. Remove from heat and set aside to slightly cool.

Meanwhile, mix the corn starch with the 2 tablespoons of cold water and set aside until ready to use.

Put the guavas and the water they boiled in into the blender and blend them on high until the mixture obtained is the texture of a liquid purée. Strain it right into the same saucepan through a fine mesh colander to collect all the seeds.

Add the evaporated milk and bring to a soft boil while gently, but constantly stirring to prevent it from burning. When the guava mixture begins to boil, reduce the heat to low and add the diluted corn starch. Keep mixing for 3 more minutes as the mixture begins to thicken. Remove from heat and add the sugar. Stir well until the sugar dissolves completely and serve immediately.

TO SERVE:

Atole is usually enjoyed either with tamales or with a variety of sweet breads such as *conchas*, *buñuelos*, sugar dusted bow ties, croissants, *polvorones*, muffins, etc.

Alternatively, you may use fresh strawberries instead of guavas.

BEAN TAMALES
TAMALES DE FRIJOL

Makes about 15, 3 ½ -inch tamales

To make the tamales, you will either need a tamale steamer or a large all-purpose steamer.

Ingredients:

15-20 dry cornhusks, softened by soaking them in water and then drained

2 cups of tortilla or tamale dough-mix (MASARICA or MASECA)

4 1/2 tablespoons of pork lard

3 tablespoons of butter

1 small white onion, sliced

1/2 cup water

1 chile pasilla

6 garlic cloves, roasted and peeled

3 1/2 cups of uncooked black beans

3-4 cups of bean broth, reserved from the cooking of the black beans

Salt & pepper to taste

TO PREPARE THE FILLING:

Cook the beans in boiling water in a large saucepan or stockpot over medium heat until the beans are soft to the touch and most of the water has been reduced, achieving about 4 cups of bean broth. Set aside.

In a frying pan, heat 3 tablespoons of butter, add the onions and fry them until golden brown. Spoon the onions into the blender jar (reserving the butter in the pan) and add the ½ a cup of water, the chile pasilla -seeds and membranes included- the previously roasted garlic and blend until smooth. Gradually, add the beans and the broth, blending well after each addition, adding more liquid only if needed to release the blades of the blender. The consistency should be that of a very thick but smooth bean purée.

Reheat the butter in the frying pan you previously used for frying the onions and add the blended bean mixture to it. Cook it over medium heat until you get a thick paste, scraping the bottom of the pan occasionally to prevent sticking and burning, for about 10 minutes. Taste and adjust the seasoning with salt & pepper if needed.

TO PREPARE THE STEAMER:

Place four dimes in the bottom of the steamer (optional). *The dimes will rattle during the cooking process while there is still water left in the bottom of the steamer; when the water evaporates, they will stop rattling, making you aware that you need to refill the steamer if the tamales are not done cooking.*

Fully cover the base of the steamer with water, and then line the steamer basket with a couple of cornhusks. Cover and place it over medium heat. Ideally, the steamer should already be warm and steaming by the time you place the tamales in it.

TO PREPARE THE DOUGH:

Work the lard and salt into the tamale dough-mix with your hands until well combined. Divide the dough into approximately 15 portions and roll each one into a ball. Put one of the smaller dough balls in the tortilla press, both plates previously lined with plastic bags on both ends and press the top plate down, but not too hard, to obtain a disk of dough of about 5 ½ inches in diameter. *Alternatively, if you don't have a tortilla press, press the dough between the palms of your hands to flatten it out or use a rolling pin.* Hold the dough disk in your hand and remove the top bag, spread a generous tablespoon of the bean paste over the center of the dough leaving a boarder of about ½ inch all around. Then, gently peel the bottom bag off and fold the dough two thirds of the way over, covering the bean filling. Then, fold the dough at each end to make a rectangular shaped pocket.

Carefully transfer the tamale to the cornhusk and cover the dough completely by folding the lower part upward first, then overlap the sides and lastly pulling the upper portion of the cornhusk down and forward. You may wish to bind it together so it doesn't fall apart and you can do it with either a piece of cooking string or a long thin piece of an extra cornhusk.

When all of the tamales have been assembled, place them horizontally in overlapping layers inside the steamer basket. Cover the tamales with additional cornhusks, close the lid tightly and cook over medium-high heat. The coins should jiggle around vigorously for about 40-60 minutes. Again, if the coins stop jiggling, it means the steamer is running low on water and more needs to be added.

When the tamales are properly cooked, the dough will be spongy and will separate cleanly from the husk. Eat them immediately or store them in the refrigerator for no longer than two days. These types of tamales freeze very well. DO NOT defrost before reheating them in the steamer.

Alternatively, try making these types of tamales with the suggested fillings: shredded cheese, cooked chicken, sautéed zucchini, green salsa, red salsa, *mole.*

You can be very creative and even pick two or more fillings but never over-stuff the tamales. You also want to make sure that the dough covers all the filling completely.

SWEET TAMALES

TAMALES DULCES

Makes about 24, 3-inch tamales

Sweet tamales are very popular in all regions of Mexico and are eaten for breakfast or dinner. They are usually accompanied with a mug of Mexican-style hot chocolate or atole. To make tamales, you will either need a tamale steamer or a large all-purpose steamer.

Ingredients for the masa (dough):

24 cornhusks (always have a few extra just in case)
soaked to soften and shaken dry

7 oz of pork lard

2 1/2 cups of tamale dough-mix (MASARICA or MASECA)

1/3 cup of water

1/2 teaspoon of salt

1 tablespoon of cinnamon

1/4 cup of sugar

2 tablespoons of grenadine syrup

2/3 cup of chopped pecans

Raisins or chopped candied fruit, pine nuts or almonds

TO PREPARE THE STEAMER:

Place four dimes in the bottom of the steamer (optional). *The dimes will rattle during the cooking process while there is still water left in the bottom of the steamer; when the water evaporates, they will stop rattling, making you aware that you need to refill the steamer if the tamales are not done cooking.*

Fully cover the base of the steamer with water, and then line the steamer basket with a couple of cornhusks. Cover and place the steamer over medium heat. Ideally, the steamer should already be warm and steaming by the time you place the tamales in it.

TO PREPARE THE DOUGH:

Put the lard in a bowl and beat it with an electric mixer until it turns very white and opaque, for about 5 minutes. Gradually beat in the dough-mix, water and salt. Beat well after each addition. Continue beating for an additional 5 minutes while gradually adding the cinnamon, grenadine syrup and the sugar. Stir in the chopped pecans.

TO ASSEMBLE:

Spread a thin, yet generous layer of dough down the middle of the husk and put a teaspoon of raisins or candied fruit of your choice on the dough. Fold the cornhusk over so that it covers the dough by folding the lower part upward first, then overlapping the sides and lastly bending the upper pointed end portion of the husk backwards and down. The overlapping tamale dough will stick and help close the cornhusk; however, you may wish to bind it together so it doesn't fall apart and you can do it with either a piece of cooking string or a long thin piece of an extra cornhusk.

When the steamer is ready, stack the tamales vertically in the steamer's basket. Cover the tamales with extra cornhusks and close the lid tightly. The coins should jiggle around vigorously for about 40-60 minutes. Again, if then coins stop jiggling, it means the steamer is running low on water and more needs to be added. Steam the tamales for about 1 hour or until the pale pink dough peels cleanly away from the husk.

Alternatively, if you don't have grenadine syrup, use ½ cup of sugar instead of ¼ cup of grenadine. This alternative method will produce off-white sweet tamales, not pink. When I make sweet tamales, I make half pink and half off-white for a stronger visual impact.

Have fun filling them creatively, but do remember to put very little filling in them because the whole point of the sweet tamales is the dough itself.

ANGANGUEO, MICHOACÁN

ANGANGUEO, MICHOACÁN

for Nikki, my daughter
"las frutas silvestres no tienen amo..." –dicho mexicano

Michoacán is a state of contrasts and magnificent beauty. People often refer to this state as being the *Soul of Mexico*. It is home to vast archeological zones, villages hidden deep within nature that seem to have frozen in time, main cities that depict rich colonial architecture, and townships full of exquisite craftsmanship.

It is also the home state to one of nature's most magnificent phenomena: the *Monarch Butterfly Migration*. Since times before time, millions of *Monarch Butterflies* have left their sanctuaries in the northern forests of the United States and Canada when the arctic cold begins to set in. Every year, between the months of October and November, they embark on a six week journey towards the south looking for a refuge away from the winter cold and a safe haven to grow, mature and eventually reproduce before heading back to the northern forests around mid-March and April. And so they find their refuge in the forests around the regions of the municipality of Zitácuaro, Michoacán.

One such forest is *el Cerro del Campanario*, a place that is easily accessed through the small, picturesque town of Angangueo.

The *Monarchs* recover from their long journey by feasting on pollen and nectar and resting, for the most part, on *oyamel* trees. These ancient and beloved insects take over every inch of the forest - the tree trunks, branches, leaves and flowers, floor, rocks, and even the people. If you happen to be in the area while this spectacle of nature is taking place, the odds are you too will turn into a part of the scenery, becoming completely covered in an ever changing tapestry of orange and black.

During pre-Hispanic times, the patterns and behaviors of the *Monarch* butterflies were a subject of study and veneration. Our ancestors documented their findings; therefore, we know that they associated the *Monarchs* with beauty and love, and that they also considered them to be auspicious. As a proof to that, fresco paintings and sculptures can be found in the multiple archeological zones that exist throughout the cities and townships of Michoacán.

Sadly, these magnificent creatures are loosing their habitat to rapid deforestation. As far as I know, although the Mexican government has implemented laws against cutting *oyamel* trees, it is still happening. Some people stop at nothing to get what they want, and others probably don't yet comprehend the devastating consequence that cutting these trees creates to this particularly fragile ecosystem.

The town and forests of Angangueo are relatively close to Mexico City. This allowed me the privilege of taking my kids –still very young at the time- on weekend trips to Angangueo and *el Cerro del Campanario* to witness this majestic display of nature, a most humbling and intoxicating experience. Once we reached the desired location, we would find a place to sit down quietly on the grass, rocks or logs, taking care to not squash any of the butterflies. We would sit there, very still, waiting calmly for butterflies to land on us and cover our bodies. Once the children got bored or it was time to leave, we would gently get up and start walking slowly in hopes that the movement would make them fly away. Some usually did and others required a bit more persuasion, but the children handled them with great care.

Upon our return to Angangueo and after cleansing ourselves of butterfly dust, grass and dirt at the hotel, we would walk a short distance to the home of a local woman by the name of Doña Rosa, who ran a *fondita*- a small homemade,

comfort food restaurant- out of her backyard. There were only about six tables dressed with colorful sarape-style looking table cloths, dispersed throughout an overgrown yard. At first sight, this was not precisely what one would consider an ideal location for eating, much less with such young children. But looks can sometimes be deceiving, and this was one such time. My kids were never very fussy eaters to begin with, but were they ever captivated by her food! So was I.

Fonditas have the characteristic of serving specific four course menus and the options are limited to what the cook wants to prepare on any given day, but really, who cares about that when everything Doña Rosa prepared was astounding. The kids would not want to eat anywhere else so you would find us there regularly enjoying the daily breakfast, lunch and dinner selections.

Some people are not very fond of sharing their recipes but Doña Rosa proved to be different; she would eagerly dictate her recipes to me as I scribbled away on a piece of paper napkin. She would pause from time to time to explain one thing or another, making sure I understood her instructions clearly. It really gives me a great deal of pleasure to be able to share a few of her recipes as part of my culinary memories.

We stopped going to Angangueo when Nikki, my youngest daughter, accidentally lost her balance and tripped, killing quite a few butterflies on her way down. Being such a kind and caring soul, the incident caused her much grief. A tremendous feeling of guilt overcame her and after that, she never wanted to return. No words of comfort and kindness were ever enough to soothe her or make her change her mind, so we began to vacation elsewhere. Since then, 15 years ago, we have not returned.

RANCHERO-STYLE EGGS

HUEVOS RANCHEROS

Serves 1

Ingredients:
2 eggs
2 tortillas
1 small tomato, whole
1/2 of a small white onion, cut in half
1 garlic clove
1 serrano chile
1 tablespoon of fresh cilantro, very finely chopped
1 teaspoon of oregano, dried and crumbled
1/2 teaspoon of powdered chicken bouillon
Vegetable oil, to fry
Salt & pepper to taste

TO PREPARE:

Roast the tomato until fully blackened, peel it completely and put it in the blender jar with the serrano chile, the onion, the garlic, the oregano, and the powdered chicken bouillon. Mix it until a smooth sauce is achieved.

Heat 1 tablespoon of the oil in a small saucepan over medium-high heat and pour in the tomato mixture. Cook the sauce for about 5 minutes or until it thickens a bit, all the time stirring to prevent it from burning. Taste and adjust the seasoning by adding salt and pepper as needed. Remove from heat and set aside until ready to use. Cover the saucepan to prevent heat from escaping.

In a small frying pan, heat 2 tablespoons of oil over medium heat until very hot. Fry the tortillas for about 15 seconds on each side and then quickly dunk each one in the sauce so they don't become soggy and arrange them on a large plate. Set aside.

Using the same frying pan, heat 1 tablespoon of vegetable oil and crack open both eggs carefully so as not to break the yolks. Cover the frying pan so the eggs can cook evenly. Ideally, the top of the yolk will turn opaque and the insides will remain uncooked.

TO SERVE:

Put both eggs over the tortillas and bathe them with the rest of the tomato sauce. Finish the dish by sprinkling finely chopped cilantro. As an alternative topping, add little pieces of raw chopped serrano chiles and onion. Serve with refried beans and warm tortillas on the side.

* *Alternatively, you can serve the eggs with both red and green salsas; in that case, instead of being called Rancheros, they are called divorced eggs.*

ENCHILADAS STUFFED WITH CHICKEN AND CHEESE IN CHILE POBLANO SAUCE

ENCHILADAS RELLENAS DE POLLO Y QUESO CON SALSA DE CHILE POBLANO

Serves 6

Ingredients:
12 fresh corn tortillas, white or blue
5 poblano chiles
1 cup of heavy cream
3 tablespoons of butter
2 chicken breasts, fully cooked by boiling
1 cup of Monterrey Jack or manchego cheese, grated
1/2 cup of fresh cheese, crumbled
1 small white onion, thinly sliced
1 small red onion, finely chopped
1 small lettuce, finely sliced
4 radishes, very thinly sliced
1 garlic clove
Corn or vegetable oil, as needed
3/4 cup of sour cream
Salt & pepper to taste

TO PREPARE:

Roast the poblano chiles, peel them completely and remove the seeds and membranes. Put them in the blender jar with the heavy cream and garlic. Mix until completely smooth and set aside.

Shred the cooked chicken breasts into a mixing bowl and add the grated cheese and the finely sliced white onion. Mix around with your hands. Set aside.

Add a scant cup of vegetable or corn oil to a medium sized saucepan and heat it over medium-high heat. Once hot, reduce the heat to medium and deep fry one tortilla at a time for about 5 seconds on each side. Set them on a plate covered with paper towels to rid them of the excess oil.

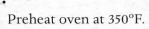

Preheat oven at 350°F.

Stuff the tortillas generously down the middle with the chicken and cheese mixture and roll them up. Place them on an oven safe container or Pyrex and set aside.

Heat the 3 tablespoons of butter in a small but deep saucepan and when hot, add the poblano chile sauce. Cook until the sauce boils, stirring constantly until it starts to thicken. Taste and adjust the seasoning by adding salt and pepper as needed.

Remove the sauce from the stove and pour it evenly over the stuffed tortillas. Bake for about 15 minutes, just long enough for the cheese inside of the tortillas to melt.

TO SERVE:

Put the sliced lettuce on the bottom of the plate. Place 2 enchiladas on top of the lettuce and garnish them with a dollop of sour cream, the crumbled fresh cheese and the finely chopped red onion. Decorate the plates with the sliced radishes (optional). Serve alongside refried beans or *frijoles de olla* - pot beans (recipe found on page 144).

RED CHILAQUILES
CHILAQUILES ROJOS

Serves 6

Ingredients:

18 corn tortillas, cut in triangles —6 pieces per tortilla
1 cup of corn oil, to fry the tortilla triangles
2 tablespoon of olive oil
2 ancho chiles, soaked in very hot water for 30 minutes, seeded and membranes removed
4 cups of water
6 tomatoes, whole
1 or 2 serrano chiles, depending on how spicy you want it
1/2 white onion
1/2 white onion, finely chopped
4 garlic cloves
1/2 cup of cilantro, finely chopped
2 chicken bouillon cubes
1 cup of sour cream
1 cup of fresh cheese, crumbled
Salt & pepper to taste

TO PREPARE:

Cut the tortillas in half and then cut each half into three pieces to form triangles.

Heat the oil in a deep saucepan over medium heat and deep fry the tortilla pieces a few at a time. *Make sure the oil is hot before frying the tortillas*. The tortillas will turn crispy and light golden brown. Use tongs or a metal spoon with holes to scoop them out of the hot oil. Transfer them to a plate covered with paper towels to rid them of the excess oil. Set aside.

Bring the two cups of water to a boil in a large, deep saucepan and dip the whole tomatoes for only 30 seconds, just to loosen the skin. Remove the tomatoes from the water, but reserve the water. Peel the tomatoes completely and return them to the boiling water and add the serrano chiles. Boil for an additional 10 minutes. Transfer the tomatoes, the chiles and the water they cooked in to the blender jar and mix well. Then add the softened ancho chiles, the onion and the garlic and blend some more until a smooth, liquid sauce is achieved.

Heat the olive oil in the same saucepan previously used over medium heat and when hot, add the tomato sauce. This process allows the flavors to combine well and for the sauce to thicken a little bit. Add the chicken bouillon and mix well. Taste and adjust the seasoning by adding salt and pepper only if needed.

When the tomato sauce begins to boil, add the fried crispy tortilla chips. Stir gently to cover them completely with the sauce. Allow the tortilla triangles to absorb the sauce for about 2 minutes before serving.

TO SERVE:

Place a generous quantity of chilaquiles on each plate. Finish the dish by adding a dollop of sour cream on top of the chilaquiles and sprinkling them with the crumbled cheese, onion and cilantro. Serve with a side of refried beans or *frijoles de olla* - pot beans (recipe found on page 144).

TORTILLAS STUFFED WITH SCRAMBLED EGGS BAKED IN A HEARTY BEAN SAUCE WITH CHORIZO

ENFRIJOLADAS RELLENAS DE HUEVOS REVUELTOS CON CHORIZO

Serves 6

Ingredients:

1 –16 oz bag of black or red beans, uncooked
12 corn tortillas
Corn oil, as needed to fry
10 eggs, beaten
8 oz of Muenster cheese, grated
1 cup of heavy cream
2 large tomatoes, cut in thick slices
1 large or 2 small ripe avocados, cut in slices
1 white onion, cut in half
1 large chorizo sausage
1 chicken bouillon cube
2 serrano chiles, chopped finely (optional)
Salt & pepper to taste

TO PREPARE:

Fill a large pot halfway with water and bring it to a boil over high heat. Rinse the beans in hot water and put them in the pot along with one of the onion halves. Cook until the beans become soft, for approximately 1 hour.

Meanwhile, chop the remaining half onion very finely and set aside.

Heat a good amount of corn oil in a medium sized saucepan over medium heat. Once the oil is very hot, fry each one the corn tortillas for about 5 seconds on each side. *The tortillas need to be soft and easy to work with.* Transfer the fried tortillas to a plate covered with paper towels to rid them of the excess oil.

Cook the chorizo sausage in a frying pan until it crumbles and is fully cooked. Transfer it to a bowl and set aside. *Reserve the chorizo fat in the pan.*

Beat the eggs and cook them in the pan containing the chorizo fat. Sprinkle them lightly with salt and pepper.

Fill each tortilla generously down the middle with the scrambled eggs and roll them up. Arrange them on a large oven safe container or glass Pyrex and set aside.

Preheat oven to 350F.

When the beans are cooked, put 2 ½ cups of the beans, 2 ½ cups of the bean broth and the chicken bouillon in the blender jar and mix well until a smooth and light bean sauce is achieved. Taste and adjust the seasoning with salt and pepper if needed.

Cover the egg-stuffed tortillas evenly with the bean sauce and then pour the cup of heavy cream in an uneven pattern. Sprinkle with the grated cheese, the onion, the serrano chiles and the cooked chorizo. Bake it for 25 minutes or so, until the cheese is completely melted and the bean sauce is slightly bubbling.

TO SERVE:

Arrange 2 enfrijoladas on each plate and serve them with a couple of slices of tomato, avocado, and homemade salsas.

POT BEANS

FRIJOLES DE OLLA

Serves 8

Ingredients:
3 cups of black beans, uncooked
1 gallon (16 cups) of water
1/2 white onion
3 tablespoons of bacon fat
1 epazote sprig (optional)
2 cilantro sprigs
4 serrano chiles
Salt & pepper to taste

TO PREPARE:

Rinse the beans in cold water and rid them of any that look wrinkled, or of any small pebbles you might encounter. Place them in a large casserole or pot, ideally clay, and fully cover them with lukewarm water. Allow them to soak for 3 to 4 hours.

Discard the water they soaked in and replace it with a gallon of fresh water. Add the bacon fat and the onion and transfer them to the stove over medium-high heat to cook, covered, for 1 ½ hours or until the beans are soft to the touch but not mushy and broken. Check them constantly during the cooking process to make sure there is always enough water covering them. If they need more water, add some, making sure it is hot water that you are adding.

When the beans are cooked and a rich bean broth has been achieved, add the epazote sprig (optional), the cilantro, and the serrano chiles. Taste and adjust the seasoning by adding salt and pepper as needed and cook for an additional 20 to 30 minutes.

TO SERVE:

Before serving, remove the chiles, the epazote and the cilantro sprigs. Plate the beans in deep soup bowls.

REFRIED BEANS
FRIJOLES REFRITOS

Serves 8

Ingredients:
4 cups of the frijoles de olla (recipe found on page 144)) with their broth
1/2 cup of bacon fat, vegetable oil or butter
1 small white onion, minced
Queso fresco, crumbled, or any other light soft cheese that crumbles such as feta (optional)
Tortilla chips, fried triangles (optional)

TO PREPARE:

Melt the bacon fat in a frying pan over medium heat and add the minced onion. Sauté it until it becomes soft and light golden brown.

Add two cups of the beans and mash them with a potato masher. Gradually add the rest of the beans with their liquid and keep mashing until you get a coarse bean paste. Keep mashing and cooking, until the beans begin to dry out. Remove from heat.

TO SERVE:

Place the beans on a platter and sprinkle them with cheese. Serve with *totopos-* fried tortilla triangles. Suggestion: If you are preparing the beans to be served with chilaquiles, reserve some of the fried tortilla chips you prepared and use them for the beans. If not, refer to the chilaquiles recipes and follow the portion that indicates how to prepare the fried tortilla triangles (recipe found on page 140).

MUSHROOM AND ZUCCHINI SOUP

SOPA DE HONGOS Y CALABACITAS

Serves 8

Ingredients:
5 tablespoons of vegetable oil
1 large white onion, finely chopped, separated
4 garlic cloves, finely chopped or minced, separated
1 1/2 cups zucchini, chopped in small pieces
2 cups or 16 oz of assorted mushrooms
8 cups of chicken broth (recipe found on page 118-119)
4 dry bay leaves
Salt & pepper to taste

TO PREPARE:

Heat 3 tablespoons of the oil in a frying pan over medium heat. Add two thirds of the chopped onion and 2 of the minced garlic cloves and cook them until translucent, taking care not to brown them. Add all of the chopped zucchini, sprinkle it lightly with salt and pepper, stir, and cook for about 3 minutes. Remove from heat and set aside.

Chop the larger mushrooms and leave the smaller ones whole. Heat two tablespoon of the remaining oil in a large saucepan over medium heat. *This is where all the soup ingredients will come together, so it must be large enough to accommodate them all.* Add the remaining chopped onion and minced garlic to the hot oil and cook them until translucent. Then add the mushrooms and increase the heat to high. Cook them for about 5 minutes, stirring constantly. Add the bay leaves and cook for an additional 2 minutes. Add the chicken broth and the sautéed zucchini. Bring the broth to a simmer over medium-low heat and cook for 10 more minutes. Adjust the seasoning by adding salt and pepper as needed. Serve very hot.

CHICKEN RED POZOLE

POZOLE ROJO DE POLLO

Serves 8

Ingredients:

1 large can of hominy

Water, as needed

8 cups of chicken broth (water reserved from cooking
the chicken and chiles in this recipe)

4.4 lbs of tomatoes, roasted

6 ancho chiles, seeded and membranes removed

6 guajillo chiles, seeded and membranes removed

4 garlic cloves

6 cilantro sprigs

3 tablespoons of vegetable or corn oil

4 full chicken breasts, uncooked

1 tablespoon of powdered chicken bouillon

6 dry bay leaves

2 tablespoons of dry oregano

1 tablespoon of dry thyme

8 corn tortillas, whole and fried

1/2 cup of vegetable oil, for frying the tortillas

4 radishes, finely sliced

1 small onion, cut in two pieces

1/2 cup of white onion, finely chopped

1/2 lettuce, finely sliced

Chile piquín or powdered cayenne pepper (optional)

4 limes, cut into 4 pieces each

Salt & pepper as needed

TO PREPARE:

In a large pot or saucepan, put the chicken breasts, the clean chiles, the cilantro sprigs, the bay leaves, two of the garlic cloves, and the onion halves. Cover with 16 cups of water and bring to a boil over medium heat until the chicken is cooked and some of the water has been reduced. At this point, don't add salt and pepper.

Meanwhile, roast the tomatoes and the remaining garlic cloves. Set aside.

Cut the limes, slice the lettuce and the radishes, and finely chop the onion to obtain ½ a cup. Set aside.

Heat the ½ a cup of oil in a small shallow saucepan. When hot, fry the tortillas one by one until they become crispy and golden brown, for approximately 30-40 seconds on each side. Transfer them to a plate covered with paper towels to rid them of the excess oil. Reserve the oil and set aside.

Once the chicken is cooked, remove it from the broth and shred it into another container. Salt & pepper the chicken lightly and mix it with your hands. Set aside.

Bring the chiles out of the broth and put them in the blender jar with the roasted tomatoes and garlic, and two cups of the chicken broth. Blend well until very smooth. *Reserve the rest of the broth for later.*

Heat the remaining oil in another large pot or saucepan over medium-high heat. Add the tomato sauce and stir in the chicken bouillon. When the tomato sauce begins to boil, add the hominy, the oregano, the thyme, and the shredded chicken. Cook for 5 minutes, constantly stirring, to prevent the sauce from burning.

Lastly, add the eight cups of the reserved broth and stir well to fully incorporate. Cover, reduce the heat to low, and allow the soup to simmer and further cook for 15 more minutes. Stir occasionally. Taste and adjust the seasoning by adding salt and pepper if needed or with more chicken bouillon.

TO SERVE:

Serve the soup in deep soup bowls. Each person will garnish their own soup with the slices of radish, lettuce, chopped onion, limes, and additional oregano. Accompany with the crispy fried whole tortillas on the side. Sprinkle with powdered cayenne pepper or chile piquín for an extra kick.

DOÑA ROSA'S
PORK CARNITAS

CARNITAS DOÑA ROSA

Serves 16

In general, carnitas are usually prepared in large quantities as it is a dish that is almost always prepared and served to large groups of people.

The following recipe serves at least 16 people; however, you can always reduce the amount of meats to suit your needs. Carnitas hold fine for about 12 days stored in the refrigerator and they reheat very well.

It is important to mention that to obtain a delicious outcome of this recipe, the meat needs to slow cook for a good amount of time. I am afraid there is no rushing this dish. Doña Rosa began preparing the recipe at the crack of dawn and the carnitas were only ready by lunch time -Mexican lunch time that is- at around 2:00pm.

Ingredients:

2 lbs of pork leg roast
2 lbs of boneless pork blade roast
2 lbs of pork shoulder
2 lbs of boneless pork loin
1 lb of pork lard (you can substitute with vegetable shortening or butter if you can't find pork lard in your local supermarket)
2 handfuls of fresh marjoram, fresh thyme and fresh bay leaves, tied
Butcher string, to tie the herbs in bundles
Water, as needed
Salt & pepper to taste

TO PREPARE:

Begin by bundling the two handfuls of herbs with the butcher string. Set aside.

Cut the meat into 3-5 inch pieces or have the butcher do it for you. Rinse the pieces of meat with water and pat them dry. Rub them with salt and set aside.

Melt the lard in a large roasting pan over high heat on the stove and add the meat. Sear the meat until very well browned on all sides. If needed, work in batches.

Preheat oven to 280°F.

When the pieces of meat have been seared, place them in a colander to drain and rid them of the excess fat. Then, add a cup of water and scrape the roasting pan with a wooden spatula to release the brown pieces that are stuck in the bottom, and without discarding this water, return the meat to the roasting pan. Add more water if needed to cover the pieces 2/3 of the way up. Add the bundle of spices, and place it in the oven.

Braise the meat in the oven, uncovered, for about 3 ½ hours. Check them once in a while and move them around and scrape occasionally, until most of the water has evaporated and the pork meat falls apart easily.

Remove the meat from the roasting pan but reserve the liquid. Once it is cool enough to handle, pull the meat apart to break it up into bit-size pieces and return it to the roasting pan. Mix it well with the remaining liquid and put it back in the oven, uncovered, until all the water has evaporated and the meat is crispy and caramelized.

TO SERVE:

Put the carnitas in a large serving platter. Accompany them with warm corn tortillas, refried beans, rice and a variety of guacamoles and red or green salsas.

POTATO CAKES

TORTITAS DE PAPA

Ingredients:
1 large egg, beaten
Vegetable oil, enough to fry
3 regular size potatoes, cooked and peeled
2 heaping tablespoons of parmesan or añejo cheese, finely grated
4 tablespoons of parsley, finely chopped
Salt & pepper to taste

TO PREPARE:

Preheat oven to 300°F.

Line both a baking sheet and a plate with paper towels.

Break up the cooked potatoes with your hands and add the cheese, parsley and egg. Adjust the seasoning with salt and pepper. Incorporate the ingredients well. Take 3 heaping tablespoons of the potato dough, make a ball and drop it carefully into the hot oil. *The oil needs to be very hot or they will get soggy and fall apart.* Deep fry them until they turn golden brown and crispy on the outside.

Put them on the plate covered with paper towels to rid them of the excess oil. Then, arrange them on the baking sheet lined with paper towels and bake them for about 10 to 15 minutes. This will allow them to dry a bit and get rid of more oil.

TO SERVE:

They are delicious when accompanied with Mexican Salsa – Pico de Gallo.

AVOCADO STUFFED WITH PORK RIND SALAD

AGUACATE RELLENO DE ENSALADA DE CHICHARRÓN

Serves 6

Ingredients:

3 large perfectly ripe avocados, halved and pitted, skin intact
1 cup of tomatoes, very finely cubed
1/2 cup of cilantro, finely chopped
2 heaping tablespoons of onion, minced
2 serrano chiles, finely chopped
1 cup of pork rinds, crumbled
1 tablespoon of lime juice, freshly squeezed
Salt & pepper to taste

TO PREPARE:

Cut the avocados in half, pit them and set aside. Be careful not to squash or damage the avocado halves as they will be used as the salad cups.

Add the rest of the ingredients to a mixing bowl, season them with salt and pepper and stir to combine well.

TO SERVE:

Put an avocado half on a plate and top each one generously with the pork rind salad. Accompany them with saltine crackers.

CORN AND HONEY TAMALES

TAMALES DE ELOTE CON MIEL

Ingredients:

22 cornhusks, softened by soaking in water

4 cups of corn kernels, cut off of the cobs

1/3 cup of honey, warmed

1 tablespoon of powdered cinnamon

1 pinch of salt

teaspoon of baking soda

TO PREPARE THE STEAMER:

Place four dimes in the bottom of the steamer (optional). *The dimes will rattle during the cooking process while there is still water left in the bottom of the steamer; when the water fully evaporates, they will stop rattling making you aware that you need to refill the steamer, if needed.*

Fully cover the base of the steamer with water, and then line the steamer basket with a couple of corn husks. Cover and place it over medium heat. Ideally, the steamer should already be warm and steaming by the time you put the tamales in it.

TO PREPARE THE DOUGH:

Put 2 cups of the corn kernels in a food processor and grind them for about 2 minutes until the kernels are broken up and their liquid has been extracted. Add the other two cups to the ones that have already been grinded and repeat the process until you obtain a soft and runny paste with some texture. Transfer the corn paste to a mixing bowl and add the warm honey, the cinnamon, baking soda, and salt. Mix well.

TO ASSEMBLE:

Put 1 to 2 heaping tablespoons of this dough down the center of a cornhusk and don't press it down. Wrap the husk loosely to allow the dough to puff up. Fold the lower part of the husk upward first, then overlap the sides and lastly, bend the upper pointed end portion of the husk backwards and down. You may wish to bind it together so it doesn't fall apart and you can do this with either a piece of cooking string or a long thin piece of an extra cornhusk.

When the steamer is ready, arrange the tamales horizontally or at an angle in the steamer. Cover them with extra corn husks and close the lid tightly. The coins should be jiggling around vigorously for about 40-60 minutes. Again, if the coins stop jiggling, it means the steamer is running low on water and more needs to be added if the tamales are not done cooking yet.

Cook the tamales for about 1 to 1 ½ hours but check them 1 hour into the cooking process to make sure they are cooking well, and that they don't over cook. They will be done when the dough turns spongy and stops being sticky. They will peel off of the cornhusk cleanly and easily.

SEASONAL FRUIT SALAD WITH PECANS IN A CREAMY DRESSING

ENSALADA DE FRUTAS DE LA ESTACIÓN CON NUECES Y ADEREZO DE CREMA

Serves 6-8

Ingredients:

3 large apples (any kind), chopped

16 oz of canned pineapple, cubed and liquid reserved

5 carrots, finely grated

1/4 cup of coconut, grated

1/4 cup of pecans, chopped

1/4 cup of raisins

1 1/2 cups of tiny white marshmallows

2 cups of heavy whipping cream

1/2 teaspoon of nutmeg

1/2 teaspoon of cinnamon

1/2 teaspoon of vanilla

1/2 cup of powdered sugar

1 cup of fresh blueberries, to garnish

TO PREPARE:

In a mixing bowl, add the apple, pineapple, grated carrots, pecans, coconut, raisins and marshmallows, and toss. Then add the reserved pineapple juice and lightly toss again. Set aside.

Beat the heavy whipping cream with the powdered sugar, vanilla, cinnamon, and nutmeg until light and fluffy.

Dress the salad with the whipping cream, toss around once more to coat evenly and transfer to a serving platter. Decorate the top of the salad with the fresh blueberries.

MEXICAN CLAY POT COFFEE

CAFÈ DE OLLA MEXICANO

Ingredients:
6 tablespoons of coarsely ground dark coffee (not instant coffee)
4 cups of water
3 oz of piloncillo or dark brown sugar
2 cinnamon sticks + 4 more to be placed in the cups (optional)
2 cloves, whole (optional)
The skin of 1/2 an orange, cut in small pieces (optional)

TO PREPARE:

In a small deep saucepan over medium heat, add the water, *piloncillo* or brown sugar, the cinnamon sticks, cloves, (optional) and orange skin (optional). Stir to dissolve the *piloncillo* or sugar and when it begins to boil, add the ground coffee and reduce the heat to low. Allow the coffee to simmer for 1 additional minute and remove it from the heat.

TO SERVE:

Strain the coffee directly into the clay pots to remove the ground coffee, cinnamon sticks, cloves, and orange skin through a very fine mesh sieve. Ideally, this type of coffee is better when served in Mexican clay pots but any ceramic or glass cup will do fine. For a visual impact, drop a cinnamon stick into the cup before serving.

CURDLED MILK DESSERT

CHONGOS ZAMORANOS

Serves 4-6

Ingredients:
8 cups of whole milk
1 rennet tablet (easily found in your local supermarket)
2 tablespoons of water
1/2 cup of dark brown sugar
2 cinnamon sticks, broken up in large pieces

For the syrup:
2 cups of water
2 cups of dark brown sugar
1 cinnamon stick, whole

TO PREPARE THE CURDLED MILK:

You will need a candy/kitchen thermometer. *Please note that it is necessary to prepare this dessert with whole milk, or else the dessert will not have the desired outcome.*

Heat the milk in a large saucepan over low heat until it reaches 122°F without allowing it to boil. *If the milk begins to simmer, stir it very gently for small intervals of time with a spoon. Ideally, you will not need to stir.*

Meanwhile, dissolve the rennet tablet in the 2 tablespoons of water. Once the milk has reached the right temperature, add the dissolved rennet. Stir well for about 30 seconds to incorporate it well. Cover the saucepan and remove it from the heat but keep it on the stove or a warm spot in your kitchen. Allow it to sit, covered and undisturbed, for about 2 to 3 hours. It will be ready for the next cooking phase when you touch it, and it doesn't stick to your finger.

Once the milk has curdled enough so that it doesn't stick to your finger when you touch it; cut large, triangular pieces with a sharp knife without removing the pieces from the saucepan. Sprinkle the curdled pieces with the brown sugar and insert the cinnamon sticks between the pieces of curdled milk. *Please note that when the milk curdles, it separates from the whey, so you will have liquid in the saucepan as well. This is exactly what needs to happen.* Cover the saucepan and return it to the stove over the lowest heat possible. Allow the curdled milk and liquid to gently simmer so as to not break up the curdled pieces. Cook it until the curdled milk is hard and has shrunk a bit, for about 3 hours. There is no need to stir, just make sure you have the heat on as low as possible. When done, remove from the heat and let cool completely at room temperature.

Remove the curdled pieces from the saucepan, cut them into smaller pieces and drain them completely of their liquid.

TO PREPARE THE SYRUP:
While the chongos are cooking, prepare the sugar syrup.

Put the water, dark brown sugar and cinnamon stick in a saucepan over medium-low heat. Stir all the time until the sugar has completely dissolved, and then allow it to simmer and reduce to about 1 cup for about 15 to 20 minutes. Stir constantly to prevent the syrup from sticking and burning. Remove from heat and set aside to cool at room temperature.

TO SERVE:
When the chongos are completely cool and drained, put them in a deep platter and cover them with the syrup. Allow them to sit in the syrup for about 1 hour before serving. They keep well for about two weeks in the refrigerator.

REAL DE CATORCE, SAN LUIS POTOSÍ

REAL DE CATORCE, SAN LUIS POTOSÍ

in memory of Doña Sabas
"el que anda en la miel, algo se le pega" – dicho mexicano

Real de Catorce was founded as a silver mining town in the 1700's and ever since then, has enjoyed quite a reputation as being a place that is difficult to access; the reason is because it is located in an extreme geographical location in one of the highest plateaus of Mexico. The drive into the state of San Luís Potosí is an uneventful one, but once you start taking the smaller roads that lead you to Real, the terrain becomes quite tricky and you find yourself driving on gravel paths and rough terrain overlooking steep, rocky cliffs. To add a little drama to the drive, you must also pass through an almost 3 kilometer long tunnel that is wide enough for only one car at a time; therefore, there are tunnel operators who determine the direction of the traffic at specific times during the day. Nighttime is not one of them; you are pretty much on your own. Although this is not the only access into Real de Catorce, the alternate route is just as challenging, if not more so. For this reason, the region remains very much untapped by tourists although I hear from my friend Bindya, who is a year round resi-

dent, that this is slowly but steadily changing. She is the owner of a beautiful, eight bedroom *hacienda*-style property that she named *Shantiniketan*, meaning Dwelling of Peace in Sanskrit. After 5 years of strenuous remodeling efforts, she turned it into a *posada* – an Inn of visitors- for those who travel to Real de Catorce in search of peace, solitude and a chance to experience nature at its best

Silver mining is not the only thing this secluded little town is famously known for. It is also a natural breeding

ground for peyote. Peyote is a grayish-green star shaped, hallucinogenic cactus that adheres closely to the earth with its thick, coned shaped roots. This cactus is very deceiving; it emanates beauty and innocence, but its flesh contains high concentrations of mescaline, a very powerful psychotropic. The word peyote comes from the Náhuatl language peyotl but it is also known as *Híkuri* by the Huichol; the Huichol are a group of ethnically indigenous people who live in southwestern Mexico and claim to have their origins in the San Luís Potosí region. Real de Catorce and its vicinity is known to the Huichol as *Wirikuta* -the sacred path- and every year, Huichol people gather to collect peyote and perform religious ceremonies to invoke the gods in the same fashion that their ancestors did.

Non-Huichol peyote seekers, who are looking for an intoxicating thrill, might soon become disappointed when they come to realize that their pilgrimage doesn't come to an end when they arrive at the gates of Real de Catorce. They still

need to either take a 4-wheel jeep ride or trek down to Estación Catorce -Station Fourteen- which is a quaint little town nestled at the foot of the valley. This is a very dangerous slope and not for the faint of heart as it is rocky, steep and narrow and only fits one of these monster vehicles at a time. Those who trek up or down this mountain are usually locals as it is not recommended for tourists. It is highly encouraged that people who drive their own vehicles into Real de Catorce park their cars, step aside and let the local experts-in-rough terrain do their thing. These "taxi" services -also known as willis - charge a nominal fee and promise to drop you off deep into the desert and collect you a few hours later.

The first time I visited Real de Catorce was in 1993. I did so with a group of 3 friends. We had been invited by a Huichol shaman to witness a ritual that invokes god *Híkuri* and to participate in a *Mitote,* which is basically a dance.

After traveling all night by bus and then enduring a very bumpy one hour ride we arrived at Station Fourteen. Station Fourteen gets its name from the local train station that just happens to be number 14. For a while, we just stood there stunned, taking in the magnificent scenery. All we could see for miles was desert vegetation, mountains, canyons and hills, the railroad, a dilapidated train station, and the modest home of a local woman who went by the name of Doña Sabas. She set us all up in one bedroom with a dirt floor and two cots with no mattresses. She looked at us and said: "This will have to do..." After putting our things down, we followed Doña Sabas into the kitchen. It was located in the patio behind the house where the fire pit clearly served as a stove. She explained how she heated her food, mentioned we should do it the same way, and then turned around and went on her merry way. After heating my canned black beans and eating them for breakfast, I strolled around the house and found Doña Sabas making Mexican string cheese.

Doña Sabas had been a lifetime resident of Real de Catorce since her birth in 1898, or so she was told. When I met her, she was short of 95 according to her own calculations. Her face was wrinkled beyond belief and her tiny frame showed signs of old age, but her charisma was that of a much younger woman. I stood besides her watching her work and listened to her explain the process of cheese making in great detail. When she was done with what she was doing she asked me: "Did you know...? I also prepare crystallized fruits and candies, I sell them at the market to make a living, would you like to watch or better yet, help these old hands?" I jumped at the opportunity to help and learn, and found myself captivated by the techniques of her candy-making craft.

The last night we spent at her home, the weather was frigid. Doña Sabas didn't seem to mind the cold; she wrapped herself in a colorful sarape, made some tea for the both of us, sat on a tree stump, and proceeded to tell me her life story. In a nut shell, I learned that she only went to school for 4 years - apparently a great achievement for a young girl in those times - she got married at sixteen to a man who liked to drink, had nineteen children but only 12 of them survived. She became a widow quite young, when she was in her forties. Her husband was drunk one evening and walked straight into the path of the train heading for Station 14, believing he could stop it. Doña Sabas and her kids just stood there, unable to do anything, watching

horrified as he took the impact that ended his life. She never remarried. And although sad to admit it, she said her life got better without him for she could now keep all the earnings she made at the market to buy food and clothing for her children, instead of the husband spending it all on booze.

Through the years, I always returned with the intention of spending more time with Doña Sabas, enjoying her company and life stories. She always kept a room in her house nice and tidy in case I'd show up, which was not as often as I would have liked. The last time I saw her was in 1999 before I left Mexico for good.

She was 101 years old when I traveled all the way to Station Fourteen to say good-bye one last time. Even then, she believed we would meet again, but we never did. During the process of trying to accurately recapture my memories for my writings, I returned to Real de Catorce and Estación Catorce with Scott and Patrick to maybe, just maybe…find Doña Sabas alive and well. As it turns out, I was a few months late.

I learned about her passing while we were waiting by the tiny plaza to take the four-wheel drive monster taxi down to the valley. We were sitting on the curb and I was talking to an older man who asked why we were going down to the valley. Were we looking for peyote? Sure we were planning to go deep into the desert to take pictures of the peyote, but I was eager to find out what had happened to the friend I left behind 8 years ago. He asked who my

friend was and I told him. "What a pity, you are a bit too late young lady; she just died a few months back. But, take solace in knowing she died peacefully at home. She died old, she was 109."

It is my wish to try to keep Doña Sabas's memory alive by telling her story and sharing a few of her recipes.

Making candy and crystallized fruit is economical, easy and fun; but it is very time consuming. The crystallizing of the fruit results from a lengthy process of cooking and dipping of the fruits in scalding sugar syrups repetitively until the right consistency is achieved. Therefore, I suggest preparing the following recipes when you have at least five hours on and off to devote to the process. It is also important to always have good ingredients, meaning the fruits you decide to prepare should be perfectly ripe, without bruises or dents or any sign that they are beginning to go bad.

Depending on the recipe to be prepared, it is important to note that if you wish to crystallize fruit skins such as limes, lemons, oranges, tangerines, and watermelon that you hollow out the pulp completely leaving the bare skin. However, if you are preparing foods such as sweet potatoes, yams, pineapple, and papaya, make sure you peel off the skin completely as well. It is very easy to crystallize figs, cherries or strawberries because they don't need to be precooked (blanched) to become soft and they don't need to be hollowed out or peeled.

When preparing crystallized fruit skins, some candy confectioners use blanching agents such as whitewash or bleach to soften and clean the skins. Doña Sabas didn't feel it necessary and therefore, neither do I, as I do believe that blanching agents may cause harm to one's health if used improperly.

And lastly, don't try to accelerate the cooking process by skipping steps; increasing the heat or failing to dip the fruits in the syrup as many times as they need to be dipped will only guarantee mediocre results.

CRYSTALLIZED LIMES WITH COCONUT CANDY FILLING

LIMONES CRISTALIZADOS RELLENOS
DE DULCE DE COCO

Ingredients to prepare the limes:
12 large limes
Cold water, enough to cover the lime skins
2 cups of sugar
1 1/2 cups of water

Ingredients to prepare the coconut candy filling:
2 cups of grated coconut, fresh is best
1 cup of coconut water, or if none is available, use tap water
1 packed cup of brown sugar
1/4 teaspoon of vanilla extract, preferably Mexican

TO PREPARE:

Cut the limes in half, scoop out the pulp and reserve for another use. Put the lime skin halves in a large saucepan and fully cover them with cold water. Bring them to a boil over medium heat. Once the water is boiling, reduce the heat to low and let it simmer for 20 minutes. Drain the lime skins and repeat the process 4 more times. *This procedure is called blanching, but done without blanching agents.* The lime skins need to be soft before being candied, so if by the time you have repeated the process 4 times the lime skins are still not soft, repeat the process as many times as needed until they are. After the last boil, rinse the limes in cold water again. Drain and set aside.

In a smaller but deeper saucepan, combine the sugar and water, mix and set over medium-high heat. Bring the mixture to a soft boil; reduce the heat to low and cover. Allow it to boil softly for 25 minutes, stirring occasionally to prevent sticking and burning. Once a thick syrup is

achieved, add the blanched limes and continue boiling, uncovered, until all of the syrup has been absorbed. Stir occasionally to ensure proper coating and to prevent burning. Remove the limes carefully from the saucepan, using tongs or a slotted spoon, and set them to dry on a cookie rack until they stiffen and hold their shape. This may take several hours.

While the limes are drying, prepare the coconut filling by combining the coconut and the coconut water (or tap water if you don't have coconut water) in a saucepan and put it on the stove over medium-low heat. Mix well and allow the coconut mixture to boil gently. Once the coconut is boiling, add the sugar. Stir well and let cook for about 30 minutes until the mixture looks and feels sticky. At this point, add the vanilla extract and mix again. When the mixture feels thick, remove from heat and let cool completely at room temperature.

TO ASSEMBLE:

First make sure that the crystallized lime skins are cold and completely dry. The lime skins should be soft, but stiff enough to be able to hold their shape. Fill each of the limes with a heaping tablespoon of the coconut filling and return them to the cookie rack to dry for at least 1 additional hour before eating them.

If you find that after filling up all the lime cups generously there is still some coconut candy left over, don't throw it out! Make small coconut candy balls using your hands, put them on wax or parchment paper and let them cool and dry completely. They make for a delectable snack.

Alternatively, dip the coconut candy balls halfway in dark chocolate.

Display on a dish or platter and don't refrigerate. This type of cooking process preserves the fruits for a very long time.

CRYSTALLIZED SWEET POTATOES

CAMOTE CRISTALIZADO

Ingredients:

4 medium-size sweet potatoes
Enough water to cook the sweet potatoes
4 cups of dark brown sugar
2 cups of water
1/4 of a tablespoon of fresh lime juice

TO PREPARE:

Peel the sweet potatoes completely. Cut them into four pieces, first lengthwise and then in half. Put them in a deep saucepan, cover them completely with cold water and bring them to a rolling boil. Once the water is boiling, reduce the heat to medium and allow them to cook, covered, for approximately 20 minutes. Remove the pieces of sweet potatoes from the water and place them on a cookie rack to cool to room temperature. The sweet potatoes should be soft, but not falling apart.

While the sweet potatoes are cooling, prepare the crystallizing syrup. Mix the brown sugar, water and lime juice in the same saucepan where the sweet potatoes were cooked, and bring it to a soft boil over medium heat stirring occasionally to prevent burning. Once the syrup begins to boil, reduce the heat to low. Add the sweet potato pieces to the syrup one at a time leaving them in there for about 3 minutes each; coating them well and evenly with the syrup. Use tongs to remove the pieces carefully and place them on a cookie rack to cool. Make sure the pieces don't touch each other while cooling. Repeat this coating process at least five times with each piece or until there is no more syrup left.

Allow the candied sweet potatoes to completely dry after the last coating for about 12 hours. The crystallized sweet potatoes should feel firm and dry to the touch and should look glossy. Display them on a dish or serving platter and don't refrigerate. Indulge yourself with them a small chunk at a time.

Alternatively, if you are crystallizing figs, cherries, strawberries, pineapple or papaya, wash them very well with cold water and set them aside to dry while you prepare the syrup. Then follow the same recipe instructions from that point on.

Cool idea: A basket full of crystallized candies makes a deliciously edible table centerpiece; they are a wonderful dessert and a great accompaniment to coffee. It is a beautiful gift, too!

MEXICAN COCONUT CANDY

COCADA DE LECHE

Ingredients:
1 whole coconut, water reserved
1 cup of coconut water, or if none is available, use tap water
1 cup of evaporated milk
1 cup of white sugar
2 egg yolks
1/4 of a tablespoon of yellow food coloring, optional
Non-stick cooking spray or vegetable oil, enough to coat the baking sheet

TO PREPARE:

Make holes in the coconut before cracking it open and reserve the coconut water in a cup.
This recipe calls for a cup of coconut water, but if the coconut doesn't have enough water to provide for a cup, use tap water to adjust the measurement.

Grate the flesh of the coconut and put it in a deep saucepan, preferably glass. Add the coconut water, the evaporated milk and the sugar. Mix well, place over low heat while constantly stirring until the coconut turns clear. Remove from heat and set aside to cool for about 5 minutes.

Add the yolks and the yellow food coloring (optional) mixing until all of the ingredients are very well incorporated and the mixture continues to cool.

Preheat oven to 350°F.

Return the saucepan with the coconut mixture to the stove over low heat, and continue mixing until all the liquid has evaporated and the mixture has become thick. Remove from heat, mix a bit more and set aside. Allow the mixture to cool completely at room temperature.

Meanwhile, lightly coat the baking sheet with non-stick cooking spray or vegetable oil.

Using your hands, first form a 3-inch ball with the coconut candy and then lightly press between your hands to make a ½ -inch thick patty. Place the patty on the baking sheet and repeat the process until all of the coconut mixture is used.

Baking time will depend on each individual oven; however, a good rule of thumb is to bake them for about 10 to 12 minutes. The cocadas will be ready when the coconut on top looks lightly toasted and it is hard set to the touch, but soft and moist inside. Baking them gives them the finishing touch and the consistency needed to not fall apart. Using a spatula, flip them over and bake them for an additional 2 minutes or until the other side is also lightly toasted. *If while you are turning them over you notice that the bottom side of the cocadas are already lightly toasted, skip the step of putting them back into the oven.* Lastly, transfer them to a cookie rack and let them cool at room temperature.

Store the cocadas in a plastic container or display them on a platter. Do not refrigerate.

GUANAJUATO

GUANAJUATO, GUANAJUATO

for Diana & Mauricio, my aunt and uncle
"de buena casa, buena mesa"-dicho mexicano

The State of Guanajuato is located in the Table Land regions of Mexico. It is a magical state rich with history, legends and traditions. Guanajuato is also considered to be the cradle of independence as this state played a major role in the Mexican Independence war of 1810.

Guanajuato's cities portray colorful Mexican and European architecture and because of the lack of proper city and road planning many years ago, the region is now a happy mistake of cobblestone roads, bridges, tunnels, tight alleyways and labyrinths, that amuse visitors and enhance the beauty of these majestic little towns and municipalities.

Guanajuato's capital city, Guanajuato, offers travelers and locals alike many exciting places and historical landmarks to visit such as *La Valenciana* and *San Ramón* silver and gold mines; the monument to *El Pípila*, a huge statue erected as a tribute to a humble miner whose courageous acts and selflessness comprise some of the most magnificent episodes in the history of Mexico; *Las Momias de Guanajuato* –an exhibit of accidental modern day mummies – that were dug up from the Guanajuato Cemetery when the family members of the deceased could no longer pay the plot tax; *El Callejón del Beso* -The Alley of the Kiss- location of a famous and tragic love legend; Guanajuato's Basilica and many others.

The city of Guanajuato is a fun place to visit year-round. It is the host location for multiple festivals and cultural events that have international recognition

such as the *Cervantino Festival* -named in honor of Miguel de Cervantes Saavedra, author of the famous literary masterpiece *Don Quijote de la Mancha*. Every year, cultural centers such as schools, universities, museums, and theaters become prime locations for exhibits, concerts, theater plays, and workshops; the city streets, plazas and gardens are also transformed into ambulatory and outdoor theaters for street performers such as mimes, clowns & jugglers, puppeteers, balloon twisters, dancers, living statues, musicians & student bands known as estudiantinas, poetry readers & story tellers.

One of my favorite cities to visit when I travel to the state of Guanajuato is San Miguel de Allende. San Miguel is widely known for being a peaceful and safe city, for its great weather year round, its rich colonial and Gothic architecture, and also for its large expatriate population. People from the United States, Canada and Europe have found a permanent home in San Miguel. Foreigners have brought a great deal of themselves and their homelands, making this city extremely diverse and multicultural.

San Miguel is similar to the city of Guanajuato in the sense that it too is one of the most important cultural destinations in Mexico. There are festivities and festivals constantly going on throughout the year. San Miguel plays host to the Arts Festival in February; the Baroque Music Festival in March; the Puppet and Hot-air Balloon Festivals in April; the Film Festival - *La expresión en corto* - in August, and Flavors of San Miguel in October. The list could go on and on.

And then there are, of course, the religious historical landmarks that shouldn't be overlooked such as the *Oratorio de San Felipe Neri* – a church with a pink cantera stone façade and baroque architecture; the *Capilla de Nuestra Señora de la Salud* – a chapel dedicated to the Virgin of Health – whose steeple houses the oldest bell in the city; and then there's the *Parroquia de San Miguel Arcángel*, a beautiful parish that is situated in front of *Plaza Allende* –also known as the main plaza or *el jardín*- that sits right in the middle of the city's downtown.

Surrounding *Plaza Allende* are numerous excellent restaurants, cafeterias and coffee shops, stunning stores, and art galleries. When I visit San Miguel, I make it a point to enjoy breakfast in one of the cafeterias under the Guadalupe or Allende Portals, overlooking the main plaza as they serve two of my favorite breakfast dishes: *Enchiladas Mineras de la Capital and Molletes*. If you get lucky enough, you might even catch a *mojiganga* parade – a giant puppet parade that interacts with people on the streets and is accompanied by an *estudiantina* –a music group- that entices spectators to dance around with the puppets to the tunes that they play.

MINER STYLE ENCHILADAS

ENCHILADAS MINERAS DE LA CAPITAL

Serves 6

Ingredients:
24 corn tortillas
Vegetable oil, to fry

Ingredients for the salsa:
25 dried guajillo chiles, seeded and membrane removed
2 garlic cloves
1 teaspoon of dried oregano
Pinch of cumin (optional)
Salt & pepper to taste

Ingredients for the filling:
3 cups of fresh cheese or queso panela, crumbled or shredded
1 large red onion, finely chopped

Ingredients to garnish:
1 whole Romaine lettuce, washed and chopped
4 cups of peeled, cooked and cubed potatoes
4 cups of peeled, cooked and cubed carrots
1 cup of queso Panela or fresh cheese, crumbled or shredded
Fresh cream, as desired
Pickled jalapeño chile peppers, as desired (see alternative recipe on page 64)
Red onions, sliced (optional)

TO PREPARE:

Soak the guajillo chiles in very hot water for 20 minutes to soften.

Meanwhile, crumble or shred the cheese and mix it with the finely chopped onion. Set aside.

Put the softened guajillo chiles in the blender jar or food processor and add the garlic, oregano and cumin. Blend until smooth but thick. Transfer this salsa to a deep dish and set aside. *If needed, add a tablespoon of water at a time, just enough to release the blender blades.*

Heat some vegetable oil in a large frying pan over medium-low heat, until very hot. *Please note that this dish doesn't require deep-frying, just make sure you cover the bottom of the pan with oil lightly, but evenly.*

Working fast and carefully so as to not break the tortillas, dip the tortillas one at a time in the salsa covering them completely and immediately frying them in the hot vegetable oil for no more than 20 seconds on each side.

Fill the fried tortillas with the cheese and onion mixture and fold them in half.

Using the same frying pan and oil you used previously to fry the tortillas, sauté the already cooked potatoes and carrots over medium-high heat until they warm up and brown lightly.

TO SERVE:

Serve 4 enchiladas on each plate; drizzle the fresh cream on top and garnish the rest of the plate with the fried vegetables, lettuce, and the pickled jalapeño chiles. If you have extra cheese left over, shred it and sprinkle it on top as well.

Mashed refried beans, rice and fried chicken are great accompaniments to this dish.

A TRIO OF PLAIN, HAM AND BACON MOLLETES

UN TRÍO DE MOLLETES DE QUESO, JAMÓN Y TOCINO

Serves 2

Molletes are simple and economical to make, yet delicious and fulfilling. It's one of my favorite Mexican comfort foods. I feel compelled to make them after a rough or long day when I get home from work and feel too uninspired to create a full meal from scratch.

PLAIN MOLLETES:

Ingredients:

4 bolillos or teleras; alternatively, use baguette or French bread
1 cup of black or red refried beans (recipe found on page 145)
8 oz of manchego, Muenster, Cheddar or any other type of cheese, grated
Red or green salsa (optional)

TO PREPARE:

Preheat oven to 350°F.

Cut open the bread by slicing it down the middle. Spread a generous amount of mashed beans on each half and top them with grated cheese.

Bake until the bread is lightly toasted and the cheese is fully melted.

Serve with homemade red or green salsa.

HAM MOLLETES

Ingredients:

4 bolillos or teleras; alternatively, use baguette or French bread
1 cup of black or red refried beans (recipe found on page 145)
8 slices of ham
8 oz of manchego, Muenster, Cheddar or any other type of cheese, grated
Red or green salsa (optional)

TO PREPARE:

Preheat oven to 350°F.

Cut open the bread by slicing it down the middle. Spread a generous amount of mashed beans on each half, add a slice of ham and top it off with grated cheese.

Bake until the bread is lightly toasted and the cheese is fully melted.

Serve with homemade red or green salsa.

BACON MOLLETES

Ingredients:
4 bolillos or teleras; alternatively, use baguette or French bread
1 cup of black or red refried beans (recipe found on page 145)
16 slices of thick cut bacon, fully cooked
8 oz of manchego, Muenster, Cheddar or any other type of cheese, grated
Red or green salsa (optional)

TO PREPARE:

Preheat oven to 350°F.

Cut open the bread by slicing it down the middle. Spread a generous amount of mashed beans on each half, add 2 slices of cooked bacon to each half and top it off with grated cheese.

Bake until the bread is lightly toasted and the cheese is fully melted.

Serve with homemade red or green salsa.

Salads are great accompaniments to molletes.

During our book-writing journey, we stayed at a beautiful small hotel with a home-like feel called Casa Crayola. Casa Crayola has only 7 casitas - little houses - all of which have been exquisitely decorated in a fashionable Mexican-style decor by owner Carly Cross.

Each casita features cable TV, wireless Internet access, and a kitchenette equipped with a microwave, small fridge, coffee maker, and cooking utensils making it the perfect home away from home. We chose to stay at this particular location because the setting allowed me to prepare food in the comfort of our casita, and for Scott to photograph the dishes immediately afterward in the colorful courtyard.

BREADED CHICKEN BAGUETTE

TORTAS DE MILANESA

Serves 6

Ingredients:
6 teleras, bolillos or 6 6-inch pieces of hard rolls or baguette bread
6 thinly flattened chicken breasts (1/8 to 1/4 of an inch thick)
1 cup of bread crumbs
2 eggs, beaten
Corn or vegetable oil to fry (you can substitute with olive oil)

Additional Ingredients:
1 large red tomato, thinly sliced
1 small onion, thinly sliced and raw or caramelized
2 cups of lettuce, shredded or finely chopped
Fresh green chiles and/or pickled vegetables such as chiles, carrots and garlic
or canned chipotle chiles
1 or 2 avocados, cut in strips
Cheese, sliced (manchego, panela, Jack or Muenster)
Mayonnaise
Mustard

TO PREPARE:

Begin by preparing the *milanesas* (breaded chicken). Coat the flattened chicken breasts with the egg and completely cover them with the bread crumbs. Heat the oil in a large frying pan over medium heat and allow the oil to get very hot before beginning the frying process. *Please note: If you fry the milanesas in anything but hot oil, they will get soggy and the bread crumbs will fall off.*

Fry the milanesas for 3 to 4 minutes on each side or until the chicken is well done. Let drain of the excess oil over a plate covered with paper towels and set aside.

Cut the bread of your choice lengthwise. Spread mayonnaise and mustard to your liking, the fried breaded chicken breasts, and have fun adding the garnish suggestions from the list above.

TORTILLA SOUP
SOPA DE TORTILLA

Serves 6

Ingredients:
6 dried guajillo chiles, seeded and membrane removed
2 dried pasilla chiles, seeded and membrane removed
12 corn tortillas
2/3 of a cup of corn oil (you can substitute with olive oil)
2 cups of tomatoes, coarsely chopped
1 1/2 cups of water
1/4 of a white onion
2 large garlic cloves
2 large springs of cilantro or parsley
4 cups of chicken broth
1 chicken bouillon cube
1/2 a cup of queso fresco, crumbled (or any cheese that crumbles)
1 ripe avocado, cut into small cubes
Sour cream
Salt & pepper to taste

TO PREPARE:

Cut the pasilla chiles into strips and set aside.

Cut 10 of the tortillas in small strips and set aside.

Heat the oil in a medium sized saucepan but reserve 2 teaspoons for later use. Working in small batches, add the tortilla strips to the hot oil and toss them around until crisp and golden, for about 1 minute. Transfer them to a plate covered with paper towels to rid them of the excess oil. When finished, set aside.

Fry the 2 remaining whole tortillas in the oil until golden and almost crispy, about 45 seconds per side. Transfer them onto the plate with the tortilla strips and set aside.

In a small skillet or frying pan, heat 3 tablespoons of the left over oil that was used for frying the tortillas over medium heat. Working in batches, add the guajillo chiles and press down

with the spatula until the chiles begin to blister for about 10 seconds per side. Transfer the chiles to a plate covered with paper towels to rid them of the excess oil. Repeat the process with the pasilla chile strips and set aside.

Put the tomatoes, 1 ½ cups of water, the onion, the garlic cloves, the chicken bouillon cube, and the cilantro springs in a large stockpot over medium-high heat. Coarsely crumble the whole tortillas and the guajillo chiles into the pot (the pasilla chiles will be used as part of the garnish later on). Bring this mixture to a quick boil, and then reduce the heat to medium-low. Cover and simmer until the liquid is almost absorbed and the chiles are soft, for about 6 minutes.

Transfer the cooked ingredients to the blender jar or food processor. Add ¼ of a cup of the chicken broth and mix it until a smooth purée is achieved.

Heat the remaining 2 teaspoons of oil in the stockpot over medium-high heat. When the oil is hot, return the tomato mixture to the stockpot and bring it to a simmer. Stir constantly until the mixture becomes thicker and deepens in color for approximately 2 minutes.

Add the remaining chicken broth and bring to a full boil. After 1 minute, reduce the heat to low and simmer for 8 more minutes to allow for the flavors to develop. Taste the soup and adjust the seasoning with salt and pepper if needed.

TO SERVE:

Serve the soup in deep soup bowls or tureens and add a handful of the fried tortilla strips to each one. Garnish with pasilla chile strips, avocado cubes, cheese, and sour cream.

DOLORES HIDALGO, GUANAJUATO

DOLORES, HIDALGO

While visiting San Miguel, we drove to an adjacent municipality called Dolores Hidalgo to spend the day. We strolled through the streets and plazas and visited the historic *Parroquia de Dolores* -Parish of Dolores- where the Cry of Independence was given by father Hidalgo, an event that would begin the movement of Independence. Dolores Hidalgo also has abundant tile and *talavera* - Mexican pottery -factories that are glad to give tours of their facilities upon request.

My favorite perk to Dolores Hidalgo and the reason it makes it high on my list of places to visit while in Guanajuato is: **ICE-CREAM**. Artisan ice-cream vendors line the plaza streets to sell their out-of-this-world creations with flavors as simple as: chocolate, coffee, strawberry, vanilla, lime, coconut, prickly pear, watermelon, melon, banana, and even more exotic tropical fruit flavors such as: fig, *zapote*, *guanabana*, and *mamey*; then there is pineapple, green apple, pistachio, almond, pine nuts, pralines, and even more unusual ones such as tequila, eggnog, fried milk, *horchata* (rice water) or *pulque* (fermented drink).But how about cheese, peanut, avocado or corn? And then there's the bizarre... fried pork rind, fish and shrimp, and yes...octopus. This extensive ice-cream menu surely satisfies every palate!

ARTISAN ICE-CREAM

for Tatiana, Camila, Isabel, Valentina & Carlota, my nieces
"de poquito en poquito, se llena el jarrito..."- dicho mexicano

Many theories exist as to which ancient civilization introduced ice-cream to the modern world. There are many speculations, but the truth remains unknown. What is known for certain is that icy sherbets have been enjoyed for thousands of years and are even mentioned in history chronicles that date as far back as the Aztec empire. It is believed that ice and snow were brought down from the *Popocatépetl* – a volcano that is in itself a legend – to be enjoyed by emperor Montezuma II and other privileged individuals.

It is also known that sherbets were more like snow-cones as the balls were formed of pure ice and snow and then topped with pieces of fruit and syrupy juices. As you can imagine, sherbets were very hard to make and to keep until refrigeration came along, making sherbets and ices simpler to make and store, sparking forth the ice-cream manufacturing industry.

Without a doubt, artisan homemade ice-cream and sherbets are much better than those commercially made. There are two important differences to mention: preparation technique and quality.

Artisan crafted ice-creams and sherbets are prepared with fresh fruits and vegetables, creams, and natural flavors such as vanilla beans, chocolate tablets or pure cacao, cinnamon springs and just the right amount of sugar. The commercially manufactured ones are made with hydrogenated vegetable oils, food colorings, artificial flavors, and the quality of the ingredients is significantly inferior, drastically altering the flavor and texture of the end result.

Commercially made ice-creams need to be continually mixed and churned for long periods of time, a process that adds air content to the mixture and makes it fluff up and expand in size; it also makes it chewy. Artisan made ice-creams, however, contain no air and therefore are not fluffy and chewy, but rather smooth and creamy.

Making ice-cream and sherbets is incredibly simple and gratifying -just wait till you try them- and I encourage you to be creative and think about your own original and exotic flavors as you begin to master the basics of the different techniques.

I've been preparing my own ice-cream and sherbets for over 15 years and have come up with quite an extensive selection of flavors. The recipes that follow are my personal favorites.

To make these ice-cream and sherbet recipes you don't need any special equipment, you just need a food processor or a blender, a fork and your home freezer.

MEXICAN CHOCOLATE ICE-CREAM

HELADO DE CHOCOLATE MEXICANO

Serves 6

Ingredients:

3 1/2 oz or 1 tablet of Mexican Chocolate such as Chocolate Abuelita or Cortéz
1 1/4 cups of whole milk
1 1/4 cups of heavy whipping cream
3 eggs yolks
1/2 cup of superfine white sugar
1/8 teaspoon of a good vanilla extract, preferably Mexican
Cinnamon sticks, for decoration and enhanced visual appearance (optional)
Dried chile piquín or cayenne powder, for decoration and an extra kick
(optional)

TO PREPARE:

Put the milk, the chocolate tablet and the vanilla extract in a large saucepan over low heat. Stir gently and constantly with a wooden spatula or a whisk until the chocolate is completely dissolved. *At this point, the milk mixture will look grainy.* Remove from heat and set aside to cool, undisturbed.

In a stainless steel bowl, whisk the sugar and the egg yolks until the mixture turns pale and thick. Slowly, add the chocolate milk mixture in a thin stream, stirring all the time with a wooden spatula or whisk until well incorporated.

Return the mixture to the saucepan and cook it over low heat for 10 minutes, stirring gently all the time. *You will notice that a thin but dense foam will form on top of the mixture, this is what needs to happen.* Then turn the heat up to medium-low for 8 more minutes or until the mixture is thick enough to coat the spoon and all the foam has disappeared. It is important to keep stirring gently and continually and to not let the mixture boil, or it will curdle and/or burn. At this point the chocolate will look creamier, darker and smoother, but will still look grainy.

Remove from heat and set aside. Allow to cool for at least an hour, stirring occasionally so it doesn't form a skin on the top. If it does form a skin, don't remove it, just whisk to incorporate it.

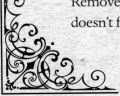

Meanwhile, whip the cream until it holds its shape and place it in the refrigerator until ready to use.

Once the custard mixture has completely cooled down, transfer it to a stainless steel or freezer-proof container and freeze it, uncovered, for 1 hour or so, until it starts to set around the edges. Remove it from the freezer and scrape and stir it with a fork until smooth and even. Now fold in the whipped cream evenly. Return it to the freezer and allow it to freeze for 2 to 3 additional hours until firm.

TO SERVE:

Serve the ice-cream balls in individual cups or cones and for a an added visual impact, stick a cinnamon sprig on the side and sprinkle the chile piquín or cayenne powder on top of it.

Alternatively, instead of Mexican chocolate tablets, you may wish to use ½ of a cup of cajeta (recipe found on page 208) or dulce de leche if cajeta is not available to you.

After the ice-cream is completely frozen, transfer it to a glass or plastic container with a lid and store it in the freezer. It is best when eaten within 2 weeks of having prepared it.

FARMER'S CHEESE WITH RAISINS AND TEQUILA ICE-CREAM

HELADO DE QUESO FRESCO CON PASITAS Y TEQUILA

Serves 4

Ingredients:
1/2 lb of farmer's cheese
1/2 cup of milk
1 1/2 cups of heavy whipping cream
1 oz of tequila
1/2 cup of raisins
1 cup of confectioner's sugar

TO PREPARE:

With a handheld mixer or whisk, beat the milk, the tequila and the farmer's cheese until well combined. *Please note: The mixture will not become completely smooth; at this point it will have a lumpy and grainy texture.* Sift the confectioner's sugar over the mixture and beat again until all of the ingredients are very well incorporated.

Transfer the mixture to a stainless steel or freezer-proof container and freeze, uncovered, for 1 hour or so, until it starts to set around the edges.

Meanwhile, whip the heavy whipping cream until it holds its shape and place it in the refrigerator until ready to use.

Remove the mixture from the freezer, scrape and stir it with a fork and mix well. Try to break apart the lumps as well as you can. Then carefully fold in the chilled whipped cream. Add the raisins and mix. Return it to the freezer and allow it to freeze for 2 to 3 additional hours until firm.

After the ice-cream is completely frozen, transfer it to a glass or plastic container with a lid and store it in the freezer. It is best when eaten within 2 weeks of having prepared it.

AVOCADO ICE-CREAM

HELADO DE AGUACATE

Serves 6

Ingredients:

2 perfectly ripe avocados, about 1 generous cup when mashed (the avocados need to be soft but firm and not have discolorations or bruising)

1 1/2 cups of whole milk

1 1/2 cups of heavy whipping cream

3 egg yolks

1/2 a cup of superfine sugar

1 tablespoon of cornstarch diluted in 1/4 cup of milk

1/4 teaspoon of salt

TO PREPARE:

In a large heavy bottom saucepan, add the milk, the diluted cornstarch and the salt. Bring to a boil over medium heat while stirring constantly but gently, to prevent from sticking and burning. Allow it to boil for 3 minutes and then remove it immediately from the heat. Set aside and let cool at room temperature, undisturbed.

Meanwhile, whip the heavy cream until it holds its shape and put it in the refrigerator to chill until ready to use.

In a stainless steel bowl, whisk the sugar and the egg yolks until the mixture turns pale and thick. Slowly add the milk mixture in a thin stream, stirring all the time with a wooden spatula or whisk until well incorporated. Transfer it to the freezer, uncovered, and allow it to freeze for about 1 hour or so, until the edges begin to set.

Wait until the cream edges set before mashing the avocado into a creamy paste. *Important: If you mash the avocado ahead of time, it will turn black and the ice-cream will not look appealing.*

Bring the mixture out of the freezer. Scrape and stir it well with a fork. Fold in the whipped cream and then the mashed avocado paste until well incorporated. Return it to the freezer, and freeze for an additional 2 to 3 hours until firm.

Alternatively, instead of avocado you may also use papaya, mamey, cooked squash or banana to prepare

this recipe. Regardless of what fruit you desire to use, make sure you get a generous 1 cup of mashed pulp.

After the ice-cream is completely frozen, transfer it to a glass or plastic container with a lid and store it in the freezer. It is best when eaten within 2 weeks of having prepared it.

PEANUT ICE-CREAM
HELADO DE CACAHUATE

Serves 6

Ingredients:
2/3 cup of shelled peanuts (whole)
1/2 cup of ground peanuts
3 vanilla beans, preferably Mexican vanilla
4 cups of whole milk
2 cups of evaporated milk
2/3 cup of heavy whipping cream
1 cup of superfine sugar

TO PREPARE:

In a large heavy bottom saucepan, add the whole milk, the evaporated milk and the vanilla beans and bring to a boil over medium heat. Once boiling, reduce the heat to low and let it simmer for 45-50 minutes. Stir occasionally to prevent burning. The liquid should reduce by half. When the milk mixture has reduced, add the sugar and stir until dissolved. Remove from heat and set aside to cool.

When the mixture has completely cooled down, cover it and place in the refrigerator to chill for a minimum of 8 hours, preferably overnight.

Meanwhile, cover the whole shelled peanuts with boiling water for about 2 minutes to clean them. Drain the water and rub off the skins if necessary. Separate the peanuts in half by pressing them between your thumb and index finger. Grind the peanuts and set aside.

Whip the heavy cream until it holds its shape and put it in the refrigerator to chill until ready to use.

When the milk mixture has chilled, strain it into a stainless steel bowl to remove the vanilla beans and then stir in the ground peanuts and mix. Transfer it to a stainless steel or freezer-proof container and freeze, uncovered, for about 1 hour or so, until the edges begin to set.

Remove it from the freezer. Scrape and stir it with a fork until even and well incorporated. Fold in the chilled whipped cream and add the halved peanut pieces. Return it to the freezer and allow it to freeze for 2 to 3 additional hours until firm.

After the ice-cream is completely frozen, transfer it to a glass or plastic container with a lid and store it in the freezer. It is best when eaten within 2 weeks of having prepared it.

CORN ICE-CREAM
HELADO DE ELOTE

Serves 4-6

Ingredients:
3 corn cobs, whole
1/2 cup of uncooked sweet corn kernels
2 cups of whole milk
1 1/4 cup of heavy whipping cream
2 cinnamon sprigs
1 teaspoon of a good vanilla extract, preferably Mexican
1/2 teaspoon of salt
3 egg yolks
1 cup of superfine white sugar

TO PREPARE:

Cut the kernels from the cobs and put them in the blender jar with the milk, the cinnamon sprigs, the vanilla extract, and the salt and mix well. Transfer the mixture to a saucepan and bring it to a boil over medium-low heat. Stir constantly to avoid burning and sticking. Once the mixture is boiling, reduce the heat to low and cook it until it begins to thicken. Remove from heat and set aside to cool.

Meanwhile, whip the heavy cream until it holds its shape and put it in the refrigerator to chill until ready to use.

In a stainless steel bowl, whisk the sugar and the egg yolks until the mixture turns pale and thick. Strain and press the corn milk mixture through a sieve to remove the corn skins and cinnamon pieces. Slowly pour the corn milk mixture into the egg yolk mixture while all the time mixing gently to incorporate well. Transfer the mixture into a stainless steel bowl or freezer-proof container and freeze, uncovered, for an hour or so, until it begins to set around the edges.

While the milk mixture is freezing, cover the sweet corn kernels with water in a small saucepan and bring it to a rolling boil over medium heat. Once it boils, cover the pan with a lid and allow the corn kernels to cook for 5 minutes. Remove from heat and drain completely, but don't rinse. Set aside to cool, uncovered.

Bring the mixture out of the freezer. Scrape and stir it well with a fork. Fold in the whipped cream. Add the cooked corn kernels and keep stirring gently until the whole mixture is well incorporated. Return it to the freezer, and freeze for an additional 2 to 3 hours until firm.

RICE PUDDING ICE-CREAM

HELADO DE ARROZ CON LECHE

Serves 6

Ingredients:

1 cup of cooked rice pudding (use the recipe found on page 76)
1 1/2 cups of whole milk
1 1/4 cups of heavy whipping cream
3 egg yolks
1/2 cup of superfine white sugar
The zest of 1 small orange or tangerine
1/4 cup of fresh orange or tangerine juice, strained

TO PREPARE:

Prepare the rice pudding and set aside to cool.

Once the rice pudding is at room temperature, put it in the blender jar with the milk, the orange or tangerine zest and the juice. Mix until the ingredients are very well combined. *Please note that the mixture will not be completely smooth.* Set aside.

Whip the heavy cream until it holds its shape and put it in the refrigerator to chill until ready to use.

In a stainless steel bowl, whisk the sugar and the egg yolks until the mixture turns pale and thick. Add the rice pudding mixture folding gently with a spatula until well incorporated. Transfer it to the freezer, uncovered, and freeze for 1 hour or so, until the edges begin to set.

Bring the mixture out of the freezer. Scrape and stir it well with a fork. Fold in the whipped cream until well incorporated. Return it to the freezer, and freeze for an additional 2 to 3 hours until firm.

After the ice-cream is completely frozen, transfer it to a glass or plastic container with a lid and store it in the freezer. It is best when eaten within 2 weeks of having prepared it.

CREAMY PASTA DE SALAMANCA SHERBET

NIEVE DE PASTA DE SALAMANCA

Serves 6

Ingredients:
1 1/4 cups of whole milk
1 1/4 cups of heavy whipping cream
3 eggs
1/4 cup of honey
1/2 cup of white sugar
1/2 cup of pulverized almonds
2 cinnamon sprigs

TO PREPARE:

Put the milk, the cinnamon sprigs and the honey in a saucepan over medium-low heat, stirring constantly, to completely dissolve the honey. Bring to a soft boil and reduce the heat to low. Cook for an additional 3 minutes. Remove from heat and immediately add the pulverized almond, mix it well and set aside to cool.

Meanwhile, whip the heavy cream until it holds its shape and put it in the refrigerator to chill until ready to use.

In a stainless steel bowl, whisk the sugar and the egg yolks until the mixture turns pale and thick. Slowly add the milk mixture, stirring all the time with a wooden spatula or a whisk, until well incorporated. Transfer it to the freezer, uncovered, and allow it to freeze for about 1 hour or so, until the edges begin to set.

Bring the mixture out of the freezer. Scrape and stir it well with a fork. Fold in the whipped cream until well incorporated. Return it to the freezer, and freeze it for an additional 2 to 3 hours until firm.

After the ice-cream is completely frozen, transfer it to a glass or plastic container with a lid and store it in the freezer. It is best when eaten within 2 weeks of having prepared it.

LEMON AND KEY LIME SHERBET

NIEVE DE LIMA Y LIMÓN

Serves 4

Ingredients:
5 medium size lemons
5 large key limes
2 cups of water
1 cup of sugar

TO PREPARE:

Zest one of the limes and one of the lemons and set aside.

Squeeze all 5 key limes and 5 lemons and set aside. Ideally, you should get about 1 ½ cups of the lemon and lime juice together.

Put the water and the sugar in a saucepan over medium-low heat and stir until all of the sugar has been dissolved. Reduce the heat to low and bring it to a soft boil, allow it to boil, without stirring, for 8 minutes to form a syrup, without letting it brown or burn.

Remove from heat and add the lemon and key lime zest; mix and set aside. Allow it to cool at room temperature for at least an hour.

When the syrup is cold, add the lemon and lime juice medley and stir until well combined. Transfer to a stainless steel bowl or glass container and freeze, uncovered, for 2 hours or so, until it becomes mushy and ice crystals begin to form.

Remove it from the freezer and scrape the sherbet with a fork to break up the ice crystals and even it out. Return it to the freezer, and freeze for an additional 3 hours until firm.

After the sherbet is completely frozen, transfer it to a glass or plastic container with a lid and store it in the freezer. It is best when eaten within 2 weeks of having prepared it.

*Alternatively, use oranges or tangerines to prepare this sherbet.

PRICKLY PEAR SHERBET

NIEVE DE TUNA

Serves 4

Ingredients:
5 green or red prickly pears
2 egg whites
1/4 cup sugar
2/3 cup of water

TO PREPARE:

Put the water and sugar in a pan over medium-low heat. Stir gently and constantly until the sugar has completely dissolved. Bring it to a boil and reduce the heat to low. Allow it to simmer without stirring for 2 minutes, then stir, and remove from heat. Set aside to cool at room temperature for at least 1 hour.

While the syrup is cooling, peel the prickly pears. *Be very careful because they have two different types of spines that penetrate the skin and it hurts if they are mishandled.* Here's how you do it: using a small pairing knife, cut lengthwise slits across the skin and peel it backwards. Discard the skins. Cut the prickly pears into fours, put them in the blender jar and don't mix, just set aside.

When the syrup is done cooling, pour it into the blender jar with the prickly pears and blend well until you get a smooth purée. Don't strain this mixture as this would remove the beautiful black seeds. Transfer to a stainless steel bowl or glass container and freeze, uncovered, for 2 hours or so, until it becomes mushy.

After the 2 hours, whisk the egg whites until they become stiff, but not dry. Bring the mixture out of the freezer. Scrape and break up the ice crystals with a fork. Fold the egg whites lightly until well incorporated. Return it to the freezer, and freeze for and additional 3 hours until firm.

Alternatively, instead of prickly pears you may wish to use kiwi, passion fruit, strawberries or pitaya.

After the sherbet is completely frozen, transfer it to a glass or plastic container with a lid and store it in the freezer. It is best when eaten within 2 weeks of having prepared it.

MANGO SHERBET WITH CHILE POWDER

NIEVE DE MANGO Y CHILE PIQUÍN

Serves 4

Ingredients:
4 large ripe mangoes
1/4 cup freshly squeezed lemon or lime juice
1/8 teaspoon of salt
2 tablespoons of powdered cayenne or chile piquín
1/2 cup sugar
2/3 cup of water

TO PREPARE:

Peel the mangoes and clean the flesh from their oblong seed right over the blender jar to catch all of the flesh and juice. Add the lemon or lime juice and salt, and blend until you get a smooth purée. Push the purée through a strainer into a stainless steel bowl, add the powdered cayenne or chile piquín and mix well. Set aside.

Put the sugar and the water in a pan over medium low heat, stirring all the time until the sugar has dissolved. Reduce the heat to low and bring it to a soft boil without stirring. As soon as it begins to boil, remove it from the heat immediately and set aside to cool slightly.

Pour the syrup over the mango purée and mix until well combined. Put it in the refrigerator to chill for about 2 hours. Immediately transfer it to the freezer, uncovered, for 2 hours or so, until it begins to form crystals and looks mushy. Scrape and break up the ice crystals with a fork. Return it to the freezer, and freeze for an additional 3 hours until firm.

After the sherbet is completely frozen, transfer it to a glass or plastic container with a lid and store it in the freezer. It is best when eaten within 2 weeks of having prepared it.

JÍCAMA AND PINEAPPLE SHERBETS WITH APRICOT-LIME SAVORY CHAMOY HOT SAUCE

NIEVE DE JÍCAMA Y PIÑA
CON SALSA DE CHAMOY PICANTE

Serves 6

Ingredients for the jícama sherbet:
2 jícamas
Juice of 2 medium-sized limes
1/2 cup of water
1/8 teaspoon of salt

Ingredients for the pineapple sherbet:
1/2 of a large fresh ripe pineapple
1/2 cup of water
1 cup of sugar

Ingredients for the chamoy sauce:
4 fresh small ripe apricots
2 cups of water
1/2 cup of sugar
3 teaspoons of corn starch diluted in 1 oz of cold water
1/2 cup of fresh lime juice
2 tablespoons of red paprika
1 tablespoon of chile piquín or powdered cayenne peppers
2 tablespoons of coarse sea salt

TO PREPARE:

Begin by preparing the jícama ice:

Cut the jícama in small chunks and place them in the blender jar or food processor. Add the water, the limes and the salt. Blend until the mixture looks between liquid and lumpy.

Pour the jícama mixture into a jell-o or any other ornamental mold of you choice. Cover it with plastic wrap and put it in the refrigerator while you prepare the pineapple ice.

Cut the pineapple into chunks and place them in the blender jar or food processor. Add the water, and the sugar. Blend until the mixture looks between liquid and lumpy.

Put the pineapple mixture in a bowl, cover it with plastic wrap and place it in the refrigerator.

Transfer the jícama mixture to the freezer, uncovered, for about an hour or so, until ice crystals begin to form.

While the jícama mixture is freezing and the pineapple mixture is chilling in the refrigerator, prepare the chamoy sauce.

Remove the pit from the apricots and put them in the blender jar or food processor with the water and the sugar. Blend them until completely liquefied and smooth and transfer into a large saucepan. Place it over low heat and add 3 heaping tablespoon of the diluted corn starch. Stir constantly until the mixture thickens. Remove from heat and set aside to cool slightly.

Once cool, transfer the apricot sauce to the blender jar again and add the lime juice, paprika, chile piquín or powdered cayenne peppers, sea salt and blend until everything is well incorporated. Taste for flavor and adjust the seasoning with salt if necessary. The chamoy sauce should taste tangy, salty, fruity, and sweet. It keeps well for about a month if refrigerated in a covered glass or plastic jar.

Once you are done preparing the chamoy sauce, check on the jícama ice. Scrape to break up the ice crystals and return it to the freezer. Transfer the pineapple container from the refrigerator to the freezer, uncovered, for about an hour or so, until it begins to freeze and form ice crystals.

Scrape the pineapple mixture to break up the crystals and transfer it onto the jícama ice mold, pressing down so as to form two distinct layers of ice flavors. Return the mold to the freezer and freeze for an additional 3 hours, preferably over night.

TO SERVE:

Flip the mold containing the sherbet onto a serving platter, drizzle the Chamoy sauce over it and then decorate the platter with lime halves. To facilitate the un-molding of the sherbet, dip the outer side of the mold in a container with very hot water, for about 5 seconds only.

Use a pie cutter or knife to cut pie-like pieces and serve in individual small flat plates. This savory-sweet sherbet is excellent as an accompaniment to cocktails.

WATERMELON AND TEQUILA ICE
GRANITA DE SANDÍA Y TEQUILA

Serves 4

Ingredients:
2 1/2 cups of diced watermelon
1/4 cup of freshly squeezed lime juice
1/4 cup of white sugar
2 oz of tequila (optional)

TO PREPARE:

Put the diced watermelon in the blender jar and mix well. While blending, add the lime juice, the tequila –if you are using it - and the sugar. You might need to work in batches.

Pour it into a glass or stainless steel container. Transfer it to the freezer, uncovered, for about 1 hour or so, until ice crystals begin to form. Remove it from the freezer and using a fork, break up the ice crystals. Cover it with saran wrap and return it to the freezer. Repeat this process at least 3 times during the freezing phase.

TO SERVE:

Scoop the watermelon-tequila ice into martini or wine glasses and decorate them with a mint leaf and/or a watermelon wedge. Be creative and enjoy!

Alternatively, instead of watermelon, you may also use cantaloupe, honeydew, pear or pineapple.

After the granita is completely frozen, if not used immediately, transfer it to a glass or plastic container with a lid and store it in the freezer. It is best when eaten within 2 weeks of having prepared it.

In the late 1980's and early 90's when my father became terminally ill, the two of us found ourselves traveling frequently to the state of Guanajuato. We would pack up our bags, scoop up my kids, who at the time were toddlers, and drive for hours until we reached our final destination: *Hotel Thermas & Spa Refugio Comanjilla*.

Comanjilla –as we call it -is located in the outskirts of a small town called Silao. It is conveniently located a mere 30 minutes away from the city of Guanajuato. Back in the 1800's, Comanjilla was neither a resort nor a spa, but rather a very humble refuge-style hotel for miners who stopped there overnight on their way to work at the mines. Soon, the word spread of this region having thermal waters with therapeutic benefits and it began to be sought out by people who because of medical ailments, wanted to enjoy the benefits of bathing in these miraculous sulfuric waters. Almost two centuries later, these springs were the reason that we too, visited Comanjilla.

The road trip to Silao would usually take us longer than normal as we did some city-hopping along the way to indulge in regional delicacies. As we drove into the state of Guanajuato, our first stop, invariably, was Celaya. Celaya is best known for its production of *cajeta*, a gooey & sticky caramel-type candy traditionally made of goats' milk. It can be eaten straight off of a spoon, but it is also used as a main ingredient in many desserts and in the manufacturing of a large variety of Mexican candies.

The consistency and flavor of cajeta varies greatly depending on the region where it is made, who makes it, the techniques involved and the ingredients used. Originally, cajeta used to be prepared only with goats' milk; today you might find that it is made with a blend of goats' and cows' milk or only with cows' milk, as goats' milk costs are becoming prohibitive and less available in certain regions.

This particular cajeta recipe calls for a blend of goat's and cow's milk but you may decide to use all cows' milk or all goats' milk. The taste and consistency will vary depending on which of the two you use, but the results are just as heavenly either way.

The recipe is inexpensive and the process is simple. Unfortunately for the not so patient ones, it does require constant mixing to avoid burning and sticking. There is no sense in trying to accelerate the process because the result will not be optimal. It helps to take turns stirring with other household members. Don't get discouraged though, because the time and effort invested in preparing this candy are well worth it, and once made, you can enjoy eating it out of the jar, spread on toast or plain María cookies, on crêpes, as a cake topping, over ice-cream, on flan and natillas, drizzled over fruits or to make cajeta jell-o (recipe found on page 307) or ice-cream.

VANILLA MILK CARAMEL FROM CELAYA

CAJETA DE VAINILLA DE CELAYA

Serves 4

Ingrediants:
2 oz of water
1 teaspoon baking soda (not baking powder)
4 cups goats' or cow's milk
1 cup of sugar
1 cinnamon stick
15 drops of vanilla extract, preferably Mexican

TO PREPARE:

In a small bowl or cup, dissolve the baking soda in the water and set aside.

Mix the milk and sugar together in a heavy bottomed pot or saucepan and bring it to a boil, without stirring, over medium heat. Once it begins to boil, reduce the heat to medium-low and while stirring constantly, add the diluted baking soda. *Take care not to pour in the sediment of baking soda that gathers at the bottom of the bowl or cup.* Then, add the cinnamon stick and vanilla extract. Continue to cook; stirring constantly with a wooden spoon or spatula, for about 1 hour or so, until the mixture thickens and coats the spoon. At this point the candy will have a rich caramel color.

TO STORE:

Cool and store in covered jars. Cajeta will keep indefinitely if refrigerated.

After treating ourselves with cajeta from Celaya, we would drive towards the city of Irapuato. The attraction: roadside strawberries. Strawberry merchants set their tents right by the highway so that travelers can stop and enjoy some delicious *fresas con crema* –strawberries with fresh cream.

Strawberry plants are not native to Mexico; they were introduced by Europeans around 1854. The climate and soil conditions of Irapuato have made it an ideal location to grow strawberries and in time, Irapuato began to harvest some of the finest strawberries in the world.

We would park our car and head directly to the strawberry stands. Sometimes, we would sit on rusty chairs around lopsided tables to eat our strawberries with fresh cream and other times, when we were more pressed for time as nighttime was approaching, we would buy them by the basketful, pick up some fresh cream in a plastic disposable cup, a little baggie of sugar mixed with cinnamon and we'd be on our way.

Typically, you cut up the clean strawberries, sprinkle sugar over them and set them aside until they have produced a fruity syrup; you add the fresh cream and done! But...what cream to use and does it make a difference? Yes, it does make a difference so let's look at the options.

Ideally, you want to get an organic, non-processed, 100% full fat, fresh cream. Fresh cream is definitely worth the calories and should be considered as choice #1. If you cannot get your hands on farm fresh cream, choice # 2 should be to use heavy cream and hand whip it yourself until it holds its shape. Choice # 3 would be to use fresh sour cream. For those watching the waistline, topping them off with yoghurt might be ideal.

The recipe also calls for sugar; you may use white, brown, or not use any at all. I never advocate the use of artificial sweeteners, but if you have an alternative diet and you are already used to them, you can use them to prepare this light dessert.

STRAWBERRIES WITH FRESH CREAM

FRESAS CON CREMA

Serves 6

Ingredients:

3 cups of strawberries, chopped in large chunks (2 cuts per strawberry)
1 cup of fresh cream (or sour cream or whipping cream)
3/4 cup of white or brown sugar, optional
Ground cinnamon, optional
Powdered cayenne pepper or chile piquín, optional

TO PREPARE:

Clean the strawberries, remove their stems, and cut them into four pieces. Place them in a bowl and sprinkle with the sugar. Stir them gently with a spoon to ensure even coverage and set aside until they release a light syrup.

If you are using whipping cream, whip it until it holds its shape. Put it in the refrigerator until ready to use.

TO SERVE:

There are several ways of serving this dish. You can add the cream to the strawberries and stir it well to ensure complete coverage or you may decide to scoop the cream on top of the berries after they've been individually plated.

At this point, sprinkle the cayenne pepper powder and/or the cinnamon. Both spices give this decadent dessert a wonderful extra kick!

Alternatively, you may wish to use a medley of berries to prepare this dessert.

Our last stop before arriving to Comanjilla was Silao's Marketplace. We would end our road trip by eating dinner at one of the market's taco stands. The ones we liked best? Taquitos de Silao, of course!

TAQUITOS SILAO STYLE
TAQUITOS DE SILAO

Serves 4

Ingredients:
16 small corn tortillas
1/2 cup of fresh cheese, crumbled
1/2 lb of chorizo, red or green
4 chipotle chiles, canned or in vinegar and cut in thin strips
1 large white or Vidalia onion, sliced
3 avocados
1/2 cup of cilantro, finely chopped
Vegetable or corn oil, enough to fry
2 limes cut in halves, optional
Green salsa
Salt & pepper to taste

TO PREPARE:

Put approximately 2 oz. of vegetable or corn oil in a large frying pan over medium heat and when the oil is hot, add the chorizos and fry them until well cooked. Remove the cooked chorizo from the frying pan and set it aside, covered, to prevent the heat from escaping.

Use the same pan with the remaining oil to fry the onions until they turn a bit darker than golden brown. Remove from the onions from the frying pan and set them aside, covered, to prevent heat from escaping.

Add a little bit more oil to the pan and lightly fry each of the tortillas on both sides until they become soft and warm.

Fill each tortilla with chorizo, and top them with fried onions, 2 thin avocado slices, a tablespoon of fresh cheese, a couple of thin slices of chipotle chiles, green salsa and a few droplets of lime juice.

TACOS

TACOS

for Daniella, my daughter
"a falta de pan, tortillas" – dicho mexicano

"Quiero inventar algo que al mismo tiempo sea plato, cuchara, servilletas y mantel - ha de haberse dicho el
inventor en el origen del proceso --, que no sea necesario lavar y que sin embargo dé a quien lo está usando la
seguridad de que lo que va a ponerse en la boca no ha pasado nunca antes por otros labios. Algo que se con-
suma al usarse, de tal manera que al terminar el banquete, sin necesidad de que nadie recoja nada, no quede
en las mesas rastro de que ahí se ha probado un bocado" —JORGE IBARGÜENGOITIA

I s there anything that hollers *Mexican* louder than the word TACOS? Every time I say the word, it not only makes my mouth water, it brings forth happy and funny memories. It doesn't matter whether you are traveling to the most recondite places of the earth or the most cosmopolitan and chic cities, people everywhere immediately associate Mexican with tacos. I remember one time when I stayed at the Krasnapolski hotel in Amsterdam. Right after checking in, the bellboy asked me: "and where exactly are you from?" I replied *Mexico,* in a moderately high, cheery voice. The hotel staff on desk-duty that morning stopped what they were doing and yelled TACOS!! in unison. It brought a smile to everyone's face and it made me laugh.

While I was growing up, my family used to spend the summer months at our vacation home in Los Angeles, California. These were the 1970's and although fast food had been around for some time in the United States, this was not an industry we had in Mexico. So my parents, my father in particular, used to take us to McDonald's and Jack in the Box, Taco Bell and a wonderful hotdog eatery called Pinks in Hollywood, and to Stan and Norm's Donuts in West Wood. My brothers and I used to get so hyper and excited about eating at these junk food joints, because they served food that was very different from the foods we were used to and provided us with alternative eating experiences. Did we enjoy it? You better believe it. Our main sin was Taco Bell. Do they serve Mexican food? No. Real tacos, chalupas or burritos? No, not even close, but we loved it.

I remember my mother's resistance to these places and her preoccupation with our health; she would look at my father and ask: "and which kinds of food have you decided to poison us with today?" So it was much to her delight that as the summer days progressed, we gradually began to ask for healthier food choices and by the end of our vacation, we were painfully craving our usual Mexican food diet. Upon our return and as soon as we walked in the door of our home in Mexico City, the table would be set and ready for us to dine on crunchy fried chicken tacos, rice and beans and other Mexican goodies prepared by Lupita, our beloved home cook.

As unfortunate as it may seem, some people believe that fast-food taco joints –which by the way I still eat at every so often- do offer real Mexican food selections, and this is absolutely not so.

So...let's chat about real Mexican tacos and what makes them such a traditional and special component of Mexican food. In modern day Mexico, we see that the nation's cuisines are still strongly influenced by the raw foods and food prepping techniques that were being used over two thousand years ago. An excellent example of this is the corn tortilla. It is by all means one of the strongest food staples of the Mexican culinary arts and it is considered a culture all by itself. Tortillas have been used in the diet of Mexicans since remote times. They provide essential nutrients in our daily diet and we use them to prepare limitless creations, not only tacos. I am, of course, referring to the authentic tortillas, those made with maize dough, pressed by hand or special machinery like those used in *tortillerías* -tortilla shops- that appear to be on every street corner throughout the Mexican republic.

When we make tacos and use fresh, soft, warm tortillas and casserole dishes to prepare them, we call them *soft tacos* because the tortillas we make are simply heated to perfection on the *comal* or a frying pan; they are not fried, crunchy or hard. The warm tortillas are then immediately filled and eaten one at a time -so they don't get cold- with the prepared meats or vegetables and garnished with fresh chopped cilantro and onion, a few drops of lime juice and we load them with fresh homemade salsas. We then move on to preparing the next taco, ideally with a different filling, garnish and salsa. This way, we get to sample the best of all worlds.

The best method of heating tortillas:
Believe it or not, the right way of heating tortillas is crucial to achieving good tacos. In México, a flat, metal cooking device called a *comal* is used for this particular process.

Heat the *comal* over high heat if you have one, or use a skillet or frying pan provided they have a flat bottom. No butter or oil is used. Once the *comal* is very hot, reduce the heat to medium. Lay the tortillas on the hot surface and use your hands to flip them at constant intervals. This process is called *throwing*. The tortillas will be ready when they are warm, soft and they have developed a slightly toasty brown color on both sides. Anything less than a perfectly well heated tortilla and you run the risk of either it breaking to pieces when you put the filling inside or tasting starchy if undercooked, or hard to roll and eat if burnt. The amount of tortillas that you can heat up at a time will depend on the size of your *comal* or frying pan.

Hard or fried tacos are also made with previously prepared meats or vegetables, but the uncooked tortillas are first filled and then rolled up and deep fried in vegetable or corn oil until the tortilla becomes crisp and golden brown throughout. These types of tacos are usually served over a bed of lettuce, topped with sour cream and accompanied with different types of salsas on the side.

I now leave you with my own translated version of one of my favorite excerpts that speaks about tacos.

"I desire to invent something that at the same time serves as a plate, a spoon, a napkin, and a table cover – must have thought the inventor while in the process of creating it-, that it is not necessary to wash and at the same time provides the user with the peace of mind that when putting it in their mouths, it has never before touched any other lips. Something that will be consumed when used in such a way, that when the banquet is over, there won't be a need for anyone to clean up and no trace will remain on the tables that people have ever eaten there".

— Jorge Ibargüengoitia

BEEFSTEAK TACOS

TACOS DE BISTEC

Serves 2

Ingredients:
6 to 8 corn tortillas
1 lb of beefsteak, cut into thin and short strips
1 medium sized onion, thinly sliced
1 green bell pepper, chopped in small pieces
6 bacon strips, chopped coarsely (optional)
6 oz of Monterey Jack cheese, grated (optional)
1 tablespoon of olive oil, *use the olive oil only if you are not using bacon
Salt & pepper to taste

Ingredients to garnish: all the garnish items are optional
1/2 cup of cilantro or parsley, finely chopped
1/4 cup of red or white onion, finely chopped
Serrano, jalapeño or chipotle chiles, chopped
2 limes, halved
Red or green fresh homemade salsas

TO PREPARE THE MEAT:

Heat a griddle or pan over medium high heat and add the bacon, the onions and the green bell peppers. Stir occasionally until the bacon looks almost cooked, and then add the beef strips. Adjust the seasoning by adding salt & pepper as needed and stir well to incorporate all flavors.

* If you are not preparing the recipe using bacon, cook the onions and bell peppers in the olive oil before adding the beef strips.

Once the meat and the bacon are fully cooked, turn down the heat to low and add the grated cheese. Allow the cheese to melt and then serve over soft, warm tortillas immediately. Finish by topping off the tacos with the suggested garnishes and a few lime drops.

FRIED CHORIZO AND POTATO TACOS

TACOS DORADOS DE CHORIZO Y PAPA

Serves 12

Ingredients:
24 corn tortillas
Vegetable oil, as needed to fry the tacos
3 lbs of white potatoes, peeled and diced
2 lbs of chorizo, casing removed
1 1/2 cups of white or yellow onion, chopped
Salt & pepper to taste

TO PREPARE THE MEAT:

Bring water to a boil and add the diced potatoes. Let them cook until soft to the touch. Drain and set aside.

Fry the chorizo and the onion in a large frying pan over medium heat. Once the chorizo is cooked, add the potatoes. Mash them and mix well. Adjust the seasoning by adding salt and pepper as needed.

TO ASSEMBLE THE TACOS:

Spread a generous tablespoon of the mashed potato-chorizo filling down the middle of the tortillas and roll them up as thin as you can get them. You may want to stick a toothpick into the rolled up tortillas to hold them together and prevent them from opening while frying.

Heat enough vegetable oil in a frying pan over medium heat and when the oil is very hot, begin to deep fry the tacos. *Please note that if you place the tacos in cold or warm oil, they will most likely fall apart.* Fry the tacos until they get an even, golden brown color throughout. Place the fried tacos on a plate covered with paper towels to rid them of the excess oil.

TO SERVE:

Serve the tacos while hot and accompany them with sour cream, avocado and salsas.

Alternatively, you may wish to not fry the tacos, in which case prepare the potato chorizo filling and heat the tortillas in a comal or a frying pan until soft and warm. Fill, roll them up and eat immediately.

SWEET GROUND BEEF TACOS WITH A PASILLA CHILE AND TEQUILA SALSA

TACOS DE PICADILLO DULCE CON SALSA DE CHILE PASILLA Y TEQUILA

Serves 12

Ingredients:
24 corn tortillas
2 lbs of 90% fat free ground beef
1 cup of white onion, finely chopped
2 garlic cloves, minced
2 tablespoons corn, canola, vegetable or olive oil, to fry
6 oz of canned tomato paste
1 packet of chicken bouillon
2 tablespoons of raisins
1/8 teaspoon of powdered cinnamon
Small pinch of powdered cloves
Cilantro, minced, to garnish (optional)
Lime, to garnish (optional)
Salt & pepper to taste

For the pasilla & tequila salsa (optional):
4 dry pasilla chiles, seeded, membrane removed and cut in small pieces
2 dry ancho chiles, seeded, membrane removed and cut in small pieces
5 garlic cloves, whole
1/4 cup of cilantro, roughly chopped
1/4 cup of olive oil
4 tablespoons of tequila
Salt & pepper to taste

TO PREPARE THE SWEET BEEF TACOS:

Heat the oil over medium-high heat in a large pan. Add the garlic and onion. When the onions become translucent, add the beef and cook while stirring constantly. When the meat is cooked half way, add the powdered chicken bouillon, the tomato paste, the raisins, and mix well to incorporate all of the flavors. Adjust the seasoning by adding a small pinch of clove, the cinnamon, and salt and pepper as needed. Keep hot until ready to serve.

TO PREPARE THE SALSA:

Heat the olive oil in a small pan over medium-high heat. Add the chiles and the garlic cloves and cook approximately for 5 minutes, stirring constantly. Transfer the pan contents to the blender, including the oil and also add the tequila, cilantro and blend well until smooth. Adjust the seasoning with salt and pepper as needed.

TO SERVE:

Heat the tortillas on a comal or a frying pan until soft and warm. Put a generous tablespoon of beef filling down the middle of each tortilla, top them off with the salsa (optional) and sprinkle them with cilantro and drops of lime juice.

CHICKEN IN TOMATO SAUCE

POLLO EN SALSA DE JITOMATE

Serves 12

Ingredients:
24 corn tortillas
6 chicken breasts or 10 chicken tenderloins, uncooked, cut in bite-size pieces
1 white onion, thinly sliced
1 white onion, cut in 4 pieces
5 large ripe tomatoes, cubed
2 garlic cloves, whole
2 packets of chicken bouillon
3 tablespoons of olive oil
1/2 teaspoon of dry oregano
2 bay leaves
Cilantro, minced, to garnish (optional)
Limes, to garnish (optional)
Salt & pepper to taste

TO MAKE THE CHICKEN IN TOMATO SAUCE:

Season the chicken lightly with salt and pepper and toss around to cover the pieces evenly. Set aside. Put the tomatoes, the 4 pieces of onion, garlic cloves, chicken bouillon, and the oregano in the blender jar and mix until liquefied and smooth.

Heat the oil in a large saucepan over medium heat and add the sliced onions and the chicken pieces. Stir constantly and allow them to cook for about 3 minutes. Then, add the tomato sauce and bay leaves; stir and cover. Reduce the heat to medium-low. Check and stir occasionally until the chicken is fully cooked and the tomato sauce has somewhat reduced and thickened. Keep hot until ready to serve.

TO SERVE:

Transfer the prepared chicken into a serving platter, warm up the tortillas on a comal or a frying pan and eat one taco at a time. Garnish with drops of lime juice, salsas, chopped onions, cilantro, and fresh or pickled chiles.

PORK RINDS COOKED IN RED SAUCE

CHICHARRÓN EN SALSA ROJA

Serves 8

Ingredients:

16 corn tortillas
2 bags of fried pork rinds, broken into approximately 1-inch pieces
1/2 small white onion
6 cilantro sprigs
6 guajillo chiles, seeded and membranes removed
3 garlic cloves
6 large, red ripe tomatoes, cut in 4 pieces
4 cups of water
2 packets of chicken bouillon
Cilantro, minced, to garnish (optional)
1 small white onion, finely chopped, to garnish (optional)
Salt & pepper to taste

TO PREPARE:

Put the tomatoes, the onion, cilantro sprigs, guajillo chiles, garlic cloves, water, and pow-dered chicken bouillon in the blender jar and mix until liquefied. You may need to work in batches depending on the capacity of your blender.

Pour the tomato sauce into a large and heavy saucepan. Put it over medium-high heat and bring it to a boil. When boiling, add the fried pork rinds to the sauce. Lower the heat to medium-low and let simmer, stirring occasionally. After approximately 20 minutes, the pork rinds will have absorbed some of the tomato sauce and will look spongy, soft and larger, and the sauce will have thickened and turned deeper in color. Taste and adjust the seasoning by adding salt and pepper if needed. Cover and remove from heat. Let stand about 5 minutes, stir, and serve immediately.

TO SERVE:

Heat the tortillas on a comal or frying pan and once the pork rinds are ready, place a generous spoonful of the pork rinds down the middle of the tortilla, sprinkle it with onion and minced cilantro. Serve alongside homemade salsas, guacamole or avocado slices.

*Alternatively, you may decide to prepare this recipe with green salsa, in which case, substitute the tomatoes for 12 tomatillos.

SHRIMP TAQUITOS
TAQUITOS DE CAMARÓN

Serves 6

Ingredients:
12 corn tortillas
1 1/2 lb of small shrimp, clean and cooked
4 garlic cloves, finely chopped
4 shallots, finely sliced
3/4 cup of cilantro, finely chopped
2 tablespoons of black sesame seeds
5 tablespoons of olive oil
2 limes, squeezed into a juice
Salt & pepper to taste

TO PREPARE:

In a large frying pan, heat the olive oil over medium-high heat. Add the shallots and the garlic and cook them until they become caramelized while all the time stirring. Add the shrimp and let cook for 4-5 more minutes, stirring well to incorporate the flavors. Add the black sesame seeds, the lime juice, the chopped cilantro, and adjust the seasoning by adding salt and pepper as needed.

TO SERVE:

Heat the tortillas and fill them up with the shrimp. Serve warm. Garnish the tacos with extra chopped cilantro, lime and homemade salsas.

PIBIL-STYLE PULLED PORK

COCHINITA PIBIL

Serves 8

Ingredients:
16 corn tortillas
2 banana leaves, softened
3 lbs of pork butt roast
1 lb of Boston shoulder
1/2 lb of achiote paste, commercially purchased
1 cup of bitter orange juice
1/4 teaspoon of dry oregano
1/4 teaspoon of cumin
1/2 teaspoon of cinnamon
1/2 teaspoon of black pepper
1 teaspoon of white pepper
6 peppercorns, coarsely ground
3 garlic cloves, minced
1/2 cup of butter or pork lard, melted
1 teaspoon cayenne pepper, powdered (optional)
Salt & pepper to taste

TO PREPARE:

The day ahead, make a marinade by mixing the orange juice, the achiote paste, the oregano, cumin, cinnamon, black and white pepper, the peppercorns, the minced garlic cloves, and cayenne pepper (optional). Place the meat cuts in this marinade and refrigerate, at least overnight.

On the day of baking, soften the banana leaves by passing them over open fire or under running hot water.

Preheat oven to 300°F.

Line a roasting pan with the banana leaves making sure there is some overhang of the leaves.

Place the marinated pork cuts in the roasting pan including ¼ cup of the marinade, pour the melted butter or lard on top of it, and lightly sprinkle it with salt and pepper. Cover it with the overlapped banana leaves and cover the banana leaves with tin foil. Place the lid on and bake for about 2 ½ hours or more, until the pork meat is very soft, pulls easily and is completely cooked. It may take longer depending on your oven capabilities.

TO SERVE:

Once the pork is fully cooked, remove from the oven and pull the pork apart completely. Taste and adjust the seasoning with salt and pepper if needed. Heat the tortillas until warm and soft and fill them up with the pulled pork. Accompany the tacos with refried beans and garnish them with fresh cilantro, chopped red onions and red or green homemade salsas. It is very popular to also top them with pickled red onions and habanero chiles.

PICKLED RED ONION AND HABANEROS:

1 large red onion, sliced
4 habanero chiles, sliced
cup of cilantro, minced
1 cup of vinegar
tablespoon of salt
tablespoon of pepper

TO PREPARE:

Place all of the ingredients in a glass jar, shake well and allow them to marinate for at least 8 hours.

POBLANO PEPPERS WITH CREAM

RAJAS CON CREMA

Serves 6

Ingredients:
12 corn tortillas
6 poblano chiles
1 cup of whipping cream
1 - 8 oz package of cream cheese
1 packet of chicken bouillon
1 medium onion, sliced
4 tablespoons of butter
Salt & pepper to taste

TO PREPARE:

Bring some water and salt to a rolling boil in a large sauce pan with a lid over medium-high heat. Add the poblano chiles and cover the saucepan with the lid. Let them boil for 6 minutes to soften, and then remove them from the heat. Discard the water and again cover the saucepan tightly for about 5 minutes so that they can steam and become easier to peel. *Alternatively, roast the chiles over open fire.*

Peel off the skin of the chiles, slice them open and discard the seeds and membranes. Then cut them into ¼-inch slices and set aside.

Melt the butter in a frying pan over medium heat and sauté the sliced onions until they become translucent and soft. Add the poblano chiles and mix. When the onions start browning, reduce the heat to low and add the whipping cream, the cream cheese and the chicken bouillon. Stir and mix to even everything out and to incorporate the flavors. Remove from heat and adjust the seasoning with salt and pepper if needed. Stir, cover and let stand for 5 minutes before serving.

TO SERVE:

Serve hot over soft and warm corn tortillas. Garnish with any homemade salsa. Rajas can also be served as a side dish.

SEASONED SCALLIONS
CEBOLLITAS

Serves 8

Ingredients:
4 bunches of scallions, whole
Olive oil, as needed
Maggi sauce, as needed
2 limes, halved
Salt & pepper to taste

TO PREPARE:

Wash the scallions, stems included, pat them dry and arrange them on a baking sheet making sure they don't overlap onto each other.

Sprinkle the scallions lightly with salt and pepper. Drizzle with olive oil and Maggi sauce to your liking and lastly, squeeze the limes on top of them.

Place the scallions in the oven and set it on broiler.

The scallions will be ready when they begin to char.

TO SERVE:

Seasoned scallions are great accompaniments to all tacos and grilled meats in general.
Alternatively, use the grill to prepare them.

SALSAS

SALSAS

for Enrique, my son
"eres más mexicano que el chile piquín" –dicho mexicano

Salsas play a big part in Mexican gastronomy and by their own right are absolute expressions of Mexican culture. A well prepared salsa is one that achieves a pleasant balance between the flavors of the ingredients used, and the heat level of the chosen chiles.

Chiles have been harvested and used since pre-Hispanic times. They were very well appreciated even back then because of their bold flavor, spiciness, and because they were considered to be appetite enhancers; not to mention their vast nutritional properties. The Spaniards who arrived during the invasion became captivated by chiles mainly because of their extensive varieties and the many ways in which they could be used; salsas were one of those uses. In the modern world, the ways that chiles are grown, prepared, consumed, dried, and ground are very similar to the ways the ancient world used to do it.

The ingredients used in Mexican salsas are very basic. Salsas usually contain either tomatoes or tomatillos -depending on the desired color, flavor and consistency of the salsa- and a combination of fresh or dried chiles, onion, garlic, cilantro, lime, salt, pepper, and sometimes avocado or other vegetables or fruits and powdered spices, in the case of sweeter salsas.

Salsas are used to accompany innumerable savory or sweet dishes, *antojitos* and *garnachas*. These food categories generally refer to *fried tacos, quesadillas, tostadas, chalupas, peneques, flautas, gorditas,* etc. These words should not be confused with the bastardizations that fast food Tex-Mex restaurants offer in their non-traditional menus.

It has been my experience that whenever Mexican food pops up in a conversation, the first thing that is usually mentioned is how spicy the food is. This statement is not necessarily true. Mexican food can be spicy if that is the desired outcome but I could argue that any kind of cuisine can be very spicy if made to be. It all depends on the personal preferences of the person preparing and eating the food.

In my opinion, a harmonious blend between ingredients is essential to achieving outstanding salsas and although I do use quite a bit of chiles in

the daily preparation of my food, the outcome is more flavorful than spicy.

I do, however, have to acknowledge that I have had, and have heard of a few horror stories involving chiles. Those of us who regularly use them in our kitchens are not exempt from the experience of being the butt of some very nasty and spicy-hot jokes made by Mother Nature from time to time. Once in a while a chile will come along that defies all expectations and my, oh my, things can heat up very fast around the dinner table... even if you do take great precaution to clean, remove their membranes and seed them properly.

It is important that when working with chiles, a few basic considerations are kept in mind. They are hot, and if you are using your bare hands to clean them and prepare them, this might not be the best time to rub your eyes. Also, some recipes call for chiles being dry roasted; this can create some unexpected fumes. If at all possible and weather permitting, open the windows or set your smoke extractor on. You'll be glad you did.

You can always control the heat level of the salsas by either adding more chiles to make a salsa spicier, or decreasing the amounts suggested in the recipes if you want a milder one without having to alter the quantities of the rest of the ingredients.

GREEN TOMATILLO SALSA WITH AVOCADO

SALSA VERDE DE TOMATILLO CON AGUACATE

Ingredients:
1/2 cup of cilantro, finely chopped
1 small onion, halved
2 ripe avocados, mashed or cubed
2 serrano or jalapeño chiles, whole
2 tablespoons of olive oil
6 fresh green tomatillos, raw and cut in four pieces
1 large garlic clove
Salt & pepper to taste

TO PREPARE:

Put the cilantro, the onion, the serrano or jalapeño chiles, the garlic clove, and the green tomatillos in the blender jar and mix well until completely smooth. Heat the olive oil in a saucepan over medium-low heat and once hot, add the tomatillo mixture. Cook for about 5 minutes stirring constantly. The sauce will turn a brighter shade of green.

Remove from heat and set aside to cool.

Once the sauce has cooled to room temperature, mash or cube the avocados and incorporate them into the tomatillo salsa. Taste and adjust the seasoning by adding salt and pepper if needed.

TO SERVE:

This salsa is used to garnish tacos, quesadillas, meats and with pork rinds or tortilla chips when served as appetizers.

ROASTED GREEN TOMATILLO SALSA

SALSA DE TOMATILLOS VERDES ROSTIZADOS

Ingredients:

½ cup of cilantro, finely chopped

1 small onion, halved

3 small garlic cloves

2 serrano or jalapeño chiles

2 tablespoons of olive oil

6 green tomatillos, raw and cut in four pieces

1/4 teaspoon of dark brown sugar

1 chicken bouillon cube

Salt & pepper to taste

TO PREPARE:

Roast the serrano or jalapeño chiles and the tomatillos on a comal or frying pan with no oil. Leave the skin on them and put them in the blender jar and add the onion, garlic, some pepper (at this point, don't add salt) and chicken bouillon. Blend until the mixture is totally smooth. Set aside.

Heat the olive oil in a saucepan over medium heat. Add the tomatillo mixture and the brown sugar and stir to incorporate well. Allow the sauce to simmer for about 5 minutes, stirring occasionally. The sauce will turn a brighter shade of green. Remove from heat and add the cilantro. Adjust the seasoning with salt and pepper if needed.

TO SERVE:

This salsa can be served hot, at room temperature or cold. To increase the levels of heat simply add more serrano or jalapeño chiles.

RAW GREEN SALSA

SALSA VERDE CRUDA

Ingredients:
6 green tomatillos, raw and cut in fours
1 large white onion, halved
2 serrano chiles, whole
2 limes
Salt & pepper to taste

TO PREPARE:

Juice the limes and set aside.

Put the tomatillos, onion and chiles in the blender jar and mix well until smooth. Add the lime juice and season it with salt and pepper.

DRIED CHILE SAUCE WITH BEER

SALSA DE CHILES SECOS CON CERVEZA

Ingredients:

10 pasilla chiles, seeded and membrane removed

10 ancho chiles, seeded and membrane removed

5 guajillo chiles, seeded and membrane removed

5 medium size tomatoes, roasted

1 small white onion

2 garlic cloves

1 packet of chicken bouillon

$\frac{1}{4}$ cup of beer

2 tablespoons of olive oil

Salt & pepper to taste

TO PREPARE:

In a large saucepan, boil the chiles with just enough water to cover them over medium-high heat. Boil them for 10 minutes to soften the chiles. Remove from heat but leave the chiles in the water. Set aside to cool.

While the chiles are boiling, roast the tomatoes and set aside until ready to use.

Put the tomatoes, chiles, onion, garlic, and the chicken bouillon in the blender or food processor and blend until smooth.

Heat the oil in a saucepan and when hot, add the sauce and cook over medium heat for about five minutes or until it deepens in color. Remove from heat and adjust the seasoning by adding salt & pepper if needed.

Once the mixture has cooled down, add the beer and incorporate well.

PICO DE GALLO
SALSA MEXICANA

Ingredients:
3 large, ripe tomatoes, chopped
1 small red onion, finely chopped
$\frac{1}{4}$ cup of cilantro, finely chopped
2 serrano chiles, chopped
Juice of half a lime (use a real lime) or a tablespoon of white vinegar
Salt & pepper to taste

TO PREPARE:

Put all of the chopped vegetables in a mixing bowl. Add the lime juice, and stir. Taste and season with salt and pepper as needed.

TO SERVE:

This salsa is a true favorite and goes well with almost anything. It is widely used on tacos, rice platters, fish, pork, red meats, and poultry. You control how spicy you want it by either leaving the chile seeds in or washing them away in very cold water if you want it milder.

Alternatively, you may wish to fry this salsa in a little bit of olive oil until it cooks, and use it to top off your fried or scrambled eggs in the morning.

TOMATILLO AND CHIPOTLE SALSA

SALSA DE TOMATILLO Y CHIPOTLE

Ingredients:
4 green tomatillos, cut in four pieces
1 green tomatillo, finely chopped
6 chipotle chiles (from a can or jar)
1 small white onion, finely chopped
4 tablespoons of olive oil
$1/4$ cup cilantro, finely chopped as a garnish (optional)
Salt & pepper to taste

TO PREPARE:

Put the pieces of the 4 tomatillos, the chipotle chiles and olive oil in the food processor or blender jar and mix until almost smooth. Transfer to a saucer and mix in the previously chopped onions and tomatillo pieces. Taste and adjust the seasoning by adding salt and pepper as needed.

TOMATO AND ANCHO CHILE SALSA

SALSA DE JITOMATE Y CHILES ANCHOS

Ingredients:

2 dry ancho chiles, without seeds, membrane removed, cut into small pieces
4 large ripe tomatoes, cut in halves
2 garlic cloves, minced or finely chopped
1 medium sized onion, chopped
3 tablespoons of olive oil
Cilantro, to garnish (optional)
Salt & pepper to taste

TO PREPARE:

Heat the olive oil in a saucepan over medium heat. When the oil is hot, add the onion, the garlic and the ancho chiles. Stir constantly until the onion and garlic are lightly brown. Don't allow the vegetables to burn. Once cooked, transfer them to the blender jar and add the tomatoes. Blend well. This sauce will not be smooth; it will have a chunky consistency. Transfer the mixture back to the saucepan and cook on medium-low for about 10 minutes. Stir constantly to prevent the sauce from sticking. Adjust the seasoning with salt and pepper as needed. Place in a bowl, cover it and chill.

TO SERVE:

This sauce is served cold or at room temperature. For an added burst of color and stronger bite, you can add serrano or jalapeño peppers at the time of blending. You can also garnish it with finely chopped cilantro and minced onion if desired.

TROPICAL FRUIT PICO DE GALLO

PICO DE GALLO TROPICAL

Ingredients:
1 cup of fresh mango, diced
1 cup of fresh pineapple, diced
1 cup of avocado, diced
1 cup red, yellow or orange bell pepper, diced
1 serrano chile, minced
$1/4$ cup of cilantro, finely chopped
3 tablespoons of freshly squeezed lime juice
$1/8$ teaspoon of cinnamon (optional)
Salt & pepper to taste (optional)

TO PREPARE:

Mix all of the ingredients together in a bowl. Make sure everything is well covered with the lime juice. Cover it and chill until ready to be served. This salsa is excellent when served alongside Brie quesadillas.

RED SALSA MADE IN A MOLCAJETE

SALSA ROJA DE MOLCAJETE

Ingredients:
2 large, ripe tomatoes
2 jalapeño chiles
2 large garlic cloves, with skin
1/4 cup of cilantro, finely chopped
Salt & pepper to taste

TO PREPARE:

Roast the tomatoes, garlic and jalapeño chiles. Transfer them immediately to the *molcajete*. Crush the roasted ingredients against the basalt stone mortar with the pestle in a twisting motion until well mixed and incorporated. You will not get a smooth sauce, but you can grind it to the consistency you desire.

Lastly, add the finely chopped cilantro and adjust the seasoning by adding salt and pepper as needed.

Alternatively, if you don't have a molcajete, you can use the blender and use the pulse button to achieve a coarser consistency.

GREEN SALSA MADE IN A MOLCAJETE

SALSA VERDE DE MOLCAJETE

Ingredients:
4 green tomatillos, raw
2 jalapeño chiles
2 large garlic cloves, with skin
1/4 cup of cilantro, finely chopped
Salt & pepper to taste

TO PREPARE:

Roast the tomatillos, garlic and jalapeño chiles. Transfer them immediately to the *molcajete*. Crush the roasted ingredients against the basalt stone mortar with the pestle in a twisting motion until well mixed and incorporated. You will not get a smooth sauce, but you can grind it to the consistency you desire.

Lastly, add the finely chopped cilantro and adjust the seasoning by adding salt and pepper as needed.

Alternatively, if you don't have a molcajete, you can use the blender and use the pulse button to achieve a coarser consistency.

EL MOLCAJETE

A *molcajete* is a stone mortar with a pestle–called *tejolote* -made of basalt or dark volcanic rock that stands on three legs for balance. It is a cooking utensil that has proven to be an essential food preparing artifact for over 6 thousand years. It is used to grind seeds, spices, herbs, chiles, and other vegetables as well as to prepare salsas. For fun, some talented artisans sculpt the outer portion of the stone to resemble certain animal heads such as: pigs, bulls, sheep, and pigeons being amongst the most common.

The blender or food processor can efficiently substitute the *molcajete* to make salsas so long as the ingredients are not over blended. Even a few extra seconds of blending can significantly alter the consistency of the salsa.

Before using a newly purchased *molcajete*, it is necessary to prepare the stone by grinding coarse sea salt and then dried corn various times, washing it with water and vigorously scrubbing it with a scouring pad. This process ensures that you will not consume pieces of stone with your salsas.

RICE AND
OTHER SIDES

RICE & OTHER SIDES

for Andrés and María
"hay de dulce, de chile y de manteca" –dicho mexicano

Rice sees its origins in Asia and has been cultivated since the beginning of civilization. It wasn't grown in Mexico until around 1591 when so many other foods and spices were introduced into the country by the Spanish conquistadores. Nowadays, rice is an essential element in every Mexican kitchen and a big part of the basic diet of the Mexican people.

Rice is a dish that can be prepared as an accompaniment to almost any other dish and can also be used in soups, stews and even desserts. In Mexico, it is very popular to top a plate of Mexican-style rice with eggs over easy for breakfast or to accompany a pork loin with white or black rice; red meats are enhanced by being eaten alongside well prepared rice casseroles topped with cooked vegetable or cactus salads and chicken dishes with yellow, green, pink or any other colorful rice dish. And it is not uncommon to make a hearty meal out of a bean and rice platter accompanied with fresh corn tortillas and salsas on the side.

My grandmother Flora used to tell me that the only way to know the difference between a good cook and a bad one is by the outcome of their rice. I acknowledge her statement as being true since it really does take skill and patience to prepare good rice. Mexican rice is characterized by being soft, fluffy, and a bit dry. Each grain holds its own as opposed to being mushy and watery. When the steps to prepare the rice dishes are followed exactly, you are likely to obtain the best results.

The secret to very good rice is to use good quality, flavorful ingredients and a bit of creativity, then to leave it alone while it cooks. *If you stir, mix or poke it during the cooking phase, you will get something that resembles a sticky wheatpaste, not good rice.* I find it helpful to cook the rice in a glass saucepan so I can tell for sure when all of the liquid has been absorbed. The next best thing would be to use a clay pot but they are not readily available for purchase in most cities within the United States.

Having a see-through lid also helps. However, if you can't tell if the liquid has been completely absorbed for any reason, stick a fork in all the way down the center and slowly pull it towards you. This will allow you to see if there is still liquid covering the bottom of the saucepan. Lastly, always remember to let the rice lay undisturbed and covered for at least 5 minutes after it's been cooked before fluffing it with a fork and eating it.

MEXICAN STYLE RICE

ARROZ A LA MEXICANA

Serves 6-8

This popular dish is usually made with vine-ripened tomatoes or good quality canned tomatoes.

Ingredients:

2 cups of white rice, unwashed and uncooked

2 cups of can peeled whole tomatoes in juice, drained or ripe fresh tomatoes

2 cups of hot water

2 packets of chicken bouillon

1/2 a white onion

3 small garlic cloves, peeled

2 tablespoons of olive oil

1/3 cup of carrot, cut into tiny pieces

1/3 cup of shelled fresh peas or frozen

6 fresh cilantro sprigs

2 to 3 serrano chiles (optional)

Salt & pepper to taste

TO PREPARE:

Mix the tomatoes, 2 cups of hot water, chicken bouillon, onion, and garlic in the blender until smooth.

Heat the olive oil in a large saucepan over medium-high heat. Add the rice and mix well coating all the rice grains with the olive oil. Once the rice starts taking a light brown color, add the tomato purée pouring it through a fine mesh colander directly into the saucepan. Make sure that the rice is completely submerged in the tomato purée, if it isn't, add more water. Stir to incorporate the ingredients and flavors and then add the carrots, peas, cilantro sprigs, chiles (optional), and stir gently. Allow the rice to boil, uncovered, for 2 minutes. Stir the rice one last time, cover the saucepan and reduce the heat to low. *Do not mix or stir the rice during the cooking process.*

Cook the rice until almost all of the liquid has been absorbed, approximately 12 minutes. Uncover, and continue to cook until the rice is tender and all the liquid has absorbed, about 10 more minutes. If the liquid is completely absorbed and the rice remains uncooked, add ½ a cup of hot water, cover it, and return it to the heat until the liquid absorbs. Repeat this process again if needed until the rice is fully cooked. Remove from heat, cover and let stand 5 minutes. Discard the cilantro and fluff the rice and vegetables with a fork. Serve immediately.

WHITE RICE CUPS TOPPED WITH CACTUS SALAD

COPITAS DE ARROZ BLANCO CON ENSALADA DE NOPALITOS

Serves 6

Ingredients for Rice:
2 cups of white rice, unwashed and uncooked
1 packet of chicken bouillon
3-4 cups of hot water
2 tablespoons of olive oil
1 garlic clove, pressed or minced
8 oz of Muenster cheese, grated
1 cup of heavy cream
Butter or oil, enough for greasing

Ingredients for the Cactus Salad:
2 cactus paddles or 1 jar of Nopalitos la Costeña
1 white onion, thinly sliced
1/2 cup of chopped up cilantro
2 tablespoons of olive oil
Maggi sauce, to season (optional)
Salt & pepper to taste

TO PREPARE:

Preheat oven to 350°F.

In a large, heavy saucepan, heat the olive oil over medium-high heat. When the oil is hot, add the dry rice grains. Mix to coat them well with the olive oil and when the rice starts taking a light brown color, add one cup of hot water. Mix and add the chicken bouillon package, squeeze the garlic with a press directly into the saucepan and mix again. At this point, add 2 more cups of hot water making sure that all of the rice is fully submerged. If it isn't, add more water.

Allow the rice to boil over medium-high heat, uncovered, for 2 minutes. Stir the rice one last time, cover the saucepan, and reduce the heat to low. *Do not mix or stir the rice during the cooking process.*

When all the water has been fully absorbed, remove from heat and check to see if the rice is soft and fluffy. If it is soft and fluffy, cover it again and set it aside for an additional 5 minutes. Fluff the rice with a fork and serve immediately.

If the rice remains partially uncooked, add ½ a cup of hot water evenly throughout, and continue to cook it over low heat, uncovered, until the water absorbs and check it again. Repeat the process if needed.

CACTUS SALAD:

While the rice is cooking, cut the cactus paddles in thin, short strips; if you are using the jarred ones, this step has already been done for you. *The cactus paddles are slimy when raw, but when they are cooked they turn moist and tender.*

Heat the olive oil in a frying pan over medium-high heat. When hot, add the sliced onions and the cactus strips. Season them lightly with Maggi sauce or salt and pepper and sauté them until they are a little over being caramelized, while all the time stirring. Remove from heat and add the finely chopped cilantro, mix well and set aside.

TO ASSEMBLE:

Fluff the rice with a fork and transfer it to a mixing bowl. Add the grated cheese, the heavy cream and stir to incorporate. Set aside.

Grease a 6 cup muffin pan or 6 individual glass or ceramic ramekins. Fill them with the rice mixture pressing down firmly, trying to pack in as much rice as you can into the molds.

Bake them for about 20 minutes or so, until the top of the rice looks moist and light golden brown.

TO SERVE:

Tilt the muffin pan upside down on the serving platter and un-mold. They will un-mold easily but if they don't, stick a fork between the mold and the rice and gently pull the rice downward. Top the rice cups with the cactus salad and serve immediately.

Alternatively, instead of topping the rice cups with cactus salad, you might wish to use a spicy cilantro sauce by following the recipe below:

TO SERVE:

Ingredients
1 bunch of cilantro
2 tablespoons of water
3/4 cup of olive oil
1 garlic clove, minced
1-2 serrano or jalapeño chiles
Salt & pepper to taste.

CILANTRO SAUCE:

Put all of the ingredients in the blender jar and mix very well until the sauce is completely smooth and uniform. Taste and adjust the seasoning with salt and pepper. Transfer the sauce into a small saucepan and cook it over medium-high heat for approximately 6 minutes or until the sauce turns a brighter shade of green, while all the time stirring.

BLACK RICE

ARROZ NEGRO

Serves 6-8

Ingredients:

3 cups of white medium grain rice, unwashed and uncooked
1 cup of hot water
2 garlic cloves, minced
2 jalapeño or serrano chiles (optional)
1 packet of chicken bouillon
2 cups of black bean broth (recipe found on page 145)
3 tablespoons of olive oil
Salt & pepper to taste

TO PREPARE:

Heat the olive oil in a large saucepan over medium-high heat. Add the rice and mix well coating all the grains with the olive oil. Once the rice starts taking a light brown color, add the 1 cup of hot water. Mix and add the chicken bouillon package, squeeze the garlic with a press directly into the saucepan and mix again. Add the 2 cups of bean broth and stir gently to combine and even out the flavors. Allow the rice to boil, uncovered, for 2 minutes. Stir the rice one last time, place 1 whole jalapeño or serrano chile (optional) into the rice, cover the saucepan and reduce the heat to low. *Do not mix or stir the rice during the cooking process.*

When all the liquid has been fully absorbed, remove from heat and check to see if the rice is soft and fluffy. If it is soft and fluffy, cover it again and set aside for an additional 5 minutes. Fluff the rice with a fork and serve immediately.

If the rice remains uncooked, add ½ a cup of hot water evenly throughout, and continue to cook over low heat, uncovered, until the water absorbs and check again. Repeat the process if needed.

TO SERVE:

Transfer the rice to a serving dish or platter and put chile strips on top of it to garnish. Mix in some whole cooked beans if some were left over from cooking the broth, but this is optional. This rice goes especially well alongside chicken or red meat dishes.

MEXICAN PINK RICE

ARROZ ROSA MEXICANO

Serves 6

Ingredients:
2 cups of white rice, unwashed and uncooked
2 tablespoons of olive oil
2 large beets, fully cooked by boiling, peeled and halved
1/2 large white onion
1 garlic clove
2 packets of chicken or vegetable bouillon
2 cups of lukewarm water
Salt & pepper to taste

TO PREPARE:

Put the cooked beets in the blender jar with the lukewarm water, onion, garlic, chicken bouillon, and mix it very well until a smooth liquid is achieved. Set aside.

Heat the olive oil in a large saucepan over medium-high heat. Add the rice and mix well coating all the grains with the olive oil. Once the rice starts taking a light brown color, add the beet water by pouring it through a fine mesh colander. Make sure the rice is completely covered with the liquid, if it isn't, add more water. Allow the rice to boil, uncovered, for 2 minutes. Stir the rice one last time, cover the saucepan and reduce the heat to low. *Do not mix or stir the rice during the cooking process.*

When all the liquid has been fully absorbed, remove from heat and check to see if the rice is soft and fluffy. If it is soft and fluffy, cover it again and set aside for an additional 5 minutes. Fluff the rice with a fork and serve immediately.

If the rice remains uncooked, add ½ a cup of hot water evenly throughout, and continue to cook over low heat, uncovered, until the water absorbs and check again. Repeat the process if needed.

TO SERVE:

Transfer the rice to a serving platter and garnish it with slices of cooked beets if any were left over. Serve it as an accompaniment to pork, chicken on red meat dishes and serve alongside warm tortillas and green or red homemade salsas.

RICE WITH VANILLA, FRIED MASHED BANANAS, RAISINS, AND RUM

ARROZ CON VAINILLA, PLÁTANOS FRITOS MACHACADOS, PASITAS Y RON

Serves 6

This savory rice is infused with vanilla beans and topped with a fried banana purée and raisins flamed with rum.

Ingredients:

2 cups of white rice
2 tablespoons of olive oil
2 cups of lukewarm water
2 packets or chicken bouillon
1 9-inch vanilla stick, cut in 4 pieces
2 ripe bananas
1 tablespoon dark brown sugar
1 tablespoon of butter
2 tablespoons of rum
4 tablespoons of raisins

TO PREPARE:

Heat the olive oil in a large saucepan over medium-high heat. Add the rice and mix well coating all the rice grains with the olive oil. Once the rice starts taking a light brown color, add the 2 cups of lukewarm water and the chicken bouillon. Make sure that the rice is completely covered with water, if it isn't, add more water. Stir to incorporate well and add the vanilla stick pieces. Allow the rice to boil, uncovered, for 2 minutes. Stir the rice one last time, cover the saucepan and reduce the heat to low. *Do not mix or stir the rice during the cooking process.*

When all the liquid has been fully absorbed, remove from heat and check to see if the rice is soft and fluffy. If it is soft and fluffy, cover it again and set aside for an additional 5 minutes. Fluff the rice with a fork and set aside.

If the rice remains uncooked, add ½ a cup of hot water evenly throughout, and continue to cook over low heat, uncovered, until the water absorbs and check again. Repeat the process if needed.

Meanwhile, heat the butter in a frying pan over medium heat and add the bananas. Mash them coarsely with a fork; add the dark brown sugar and the raisins. Sauté the banana purée until it begins to turn toasty brown in some areas. Add the rum, remove it from the heat and flame it with a kitchen torch. Set aside until ready to use. **Flambéing the banana is optional.*

TO SERVE:

Fluff the rice again with a fork and transfer it to a serving platter. Top the rice with the flamed banana purée and serve immediately.

DRUNKEN BEANS

FRIJOLES BORRACHOS

Serves 6

Ingredients:
2 cups of black beans, rinsed
16 cups of water, to cook the beans in
8 slices of bacon, chopped
1 carrot, chopped
1 large tomato, diced and without seeds
1 celery stick, cut in 4 pieces
1 small onion, quartered
1 small onion, very finely chopped
2 bay leaves, dry
2 garlic cloves, cut in 4 pieces each
2 packets of chicken bouillon
1 (6 oz) Coronita or pale lager beer
5 parsley sprigs
Salt & pepper to taste

TO PREPARE:

Bring the beans, the carrots, the quartered onions, the garlic, the parsley sprigs, and the bay leaves to a rolling boil, covered, in a large pot over medium heat. Make sure the ingredients are completely covered with water. Once it boils, reduce the heat to medium-low and allow the beans to fully cook. Check once in a while to stir and make sure that there is still enough liquid remaining.

After about two hours or when the beans are soft to the touch and the liquid has thickened and turned a deep rich dark color, reduce the heat to low. Fry the bacon with the finely chopped onion and when the bacon is fully cooked, add the diced tomato, chicken bouillon and the beer. Cook for an additional 2 minutes. Set aside.

Remove the bay leafs, the parsley sprigs, the celery, and the onion from the bean broth and discard. Immediately add the bacon mixture. Stir for an additional 3 minutes to incorporate the flavors and adjust the seasoning by adding salt and pepper if needed. Again increase the heat to medium-low and cook the beans for an additional 20 minutes.

TO SERVE:

Beans make great side dishes to almost anything and are delicious as a standalone meal. Serve them alongside tortillas and homemade salsas.

SAUTÉED BABY POTATOES

PAPITAS DE CAMBRAY

Serves 6

Ingredients:

2 lbs of yellow or red baby potatoes, rinsed
1 large white onion, minced
2 garlic cloves, minced
2 serrano chiles (optional), sliced
1/2 cup of cilantro, minced
4 tablespoons of butter
Salt & pepper to taste

TO PREPARE:

Boil the whole potatoes with their skin until soft, but don't over cook. When done, drain and allow them to cool and dry at room temperature. When cool, cut each of them into 4 lengthwise pieces and set aside.

Melt the butter in a large frying pan over medium-low heat and add the serrano chiles, onion and garlic and cook until the onion is golden brown. Add the potatoes, the cilantro and incorporate all the ingredients by constantly stirring to prevent the vegetables from sticking to the bottom of the frying pan. Adjust the seasoning by adding salt and pepper if needed. After about 15 minutes, the potatoes should be lightly caramelized, and slightly crispy around the edges but soft in the middle. Serve immediately

MEXICAN-STYLE POTATO SALAD

ENSALADA DE PAPA ESTILO MEXICANO

Serves 8

Ingredients:
10 large yellow potatoes
1 chorizo sausage
1 carrot, shredded
1/2 cup of parsley or cilantro, minced
1 small red onion, sliced finely
2 serrano or jalapeño chiles, finely sliced (optional)
Salt & pepper to taste

Ingredients for the Mayonnaise Dressing:
1 cup (or more) of mayonnaise
1 teaspoon of powdered mustard
1 teaspoon of red paprika
Pinch of cumin
2 tablespoons of Worcestershire Sauce

TO PREPARE:

Boil the potatoes and once cooked, peel and dice them. Put them in a mixing bowl and set aside.

In a frying pan over medium heat, cook the chorizo, the thinly sliced onion and the chiles (optional).

Prepare the mayonnaise dressing by whisking all of the dressing ingredients together until well combined.

Add the chorizo mixture, the minced parsley and the shredded carrot to the potatoes and incorporate well. Lastly, add the mayonnaise dressing. Make sure all of the ingredients are well covered. Adjust the seasoning by adding salt and pepper as needed.

AZTEC SALAD
ENSALADA AZTECA

Serves 4

Ingredients for the Salad:
1 cup of black beans, fully cooked
1 cup of corn grains, fully cooked
4 scallions, including stems,
finely chopped
1 large green bell pepper, chopped
1 - 2 jalapeño peppers, depending on
how hot you want it, chopped
2 tablespoons of cilantro, minced
Olive oil, as needed
1 teaspoon of oregano, dry
Salt & pepper to taste

Ingredients to Garnish:
1/2 Iceberg lettuce, washed and
well dried
3 medium size tomatoes, cut in 4
pieces
lengthwise (optional)
1 avocado, sliced (optional)
Cilantro sprigs, whole (optional)
4 corn tortillas, cut into thin and
small strips and fried in vegetable
or canola oil

TO PREPARE:

Before starting to assemble the salad, the black beans and corn need to be fully cooked.

Cut the tortillas into thin, small pieces and fry them until golden and crisp in the oil. Rid them of the excess oil by setting them aside on a plate covered with paper towels.

Put the beans, corn grains, chopped scallions and stems, green bell pepper, jalapeno peppers, and cilantro in a mixing bowl and sprinkle them lightly with salt & pepper, the oregano, and a drizzle of olive oil. Toss well to incorporate all of the ingredients and flavors.

TO ASSEMBLE:

Arrange the whole lettuce leaves on the bottom of a flat serving platter. Arrange the tomato pieces and avacado slices in the outer portion of platter. Place the bean & corn mixture in the middle of the platter and randomly scatter the fried tortilla strips over the whole salad and then garnish it with the cilantro sprigs.

MIXED GREEN SALAD WITH WALNUTS AND FRUITS IN A PINK ROSE VINAIGRETTE

ENSALADA DE LECHUGAS MIXTAS, NUECES Y FRUTAS CON ADEREZO DE ROSAS

Serves 6

Ingredients for the Salad:
The leaves of 3 whole endives, washed and dry
1/2 lb of baby green spinach, whole, washed and dry
1 small Boston lettuce, chopped, washed and dry
1 cup of walnuts
1 cup of dried cranberries
4 oranges or tangerines, peeled and in wedges

Ingredients for the Vinaigrette:
2 pink or white rose petals, washed
1/4 cup of peanut oil
1/4 cup of olive oil
1/2 cup of honey
1/2 cup of red wine vinegar
1 teaspoon of thyme
Salt & pepper to taste

TO PREPARE THE SALAD:

Arrange the salad ingredients in the following order. The endive leaves should surround the outer side of a flat serving platter, the stem sides should face towards the center of the platter. The baby spinach should go in the center of the platter, almost covering the white portion of the endives. The chopped pieces of the Boston lettuce should be scattered on top of the spinach. Lastly, sprinkle with the walnuts, cranberries and decorate with wedges of orange or tangerine.

TO PREPARE THE VINAIGRETTE:

Put all of the ingredients of the vinaigrette, except the salt and pepper, in the blender jar and mix on high for about 2 minutes or so, until a smooth and uniform sauce is achieved. Adjust the seasoning with salt and pepper if needed. Serve the vinaigrette on the side.

SHRIMP SALAD IN PURPLE CABBAGE CUPS WITH GUAVA DRESSING

ENSALADA DE CAMARONES EN COPITAS DE COL MORADA CON ADEREZO DE GUAYABA

Serves 4

Ingredients:
1 lb of cooked shrimp,
thawed, clean,
deveined and tail removed
1 small purple cabbage, 12 whole leaves
and the rest finely chopped
1 carrot, grated
1/2 cup of fresh cilantro or parsley,
finely chopped
Sesame seeds, white or black

Ingredients for the dressing:
7 guavas, canned and without
the seeds
1/2 cup of cider vinegar
1 cup of olive oil
1 tablespoon of dark brown sugar
1/2 cup of heavy whipping cream
1 1/2 tablespoon of chicken bouillon,
granulated

TO PREPARE THE SALAD:

Put the shrimp, the chopped purple cabbage, grated carrots, and the chopped cilantro/parsley in a mixing bowl. Mix well and set aside.

TO PREPARE THE GUAVA DRESSING:

Mix the guavas with the cider vinegar, olive oil and sugar in the blender until you obtain a smooth purée. When the guava mixture is completely smooth, add the chicken bouillon granules and the heavy cream and blend again just until well incorporated.

TO ASSEMBLE:

Add the guava dressing to the shrimp salad and toss to coat evenly. Adjust the seasoning with salt and pepper if needed. Stuff each cabbage leaf with the salad and serve immediately.

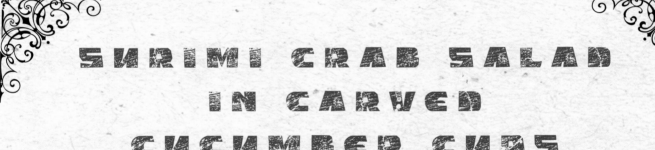

SURIMI CRAB SALAD IN CARVED CUCUMBER CUPS

ENSALADA DE SURIMI EN COPITAS DE PEPINO

Serves 6

Ingredients:

2 long cucumbers or 4 regular size ones, peeled and cut into 1-inch pieces
2 packages of imitation crab meat, finely chopped
1 small tomato, finely chopped
1/2 small onion, finely chopped
2/3 cup of fresh cilantro, minced
2 tablespoons of fresh parsley, minced
1 ripe avocado, mashed
3 generous scoops of mayonnaise
Salt & pepper

TO PREPARE:

Scoop out ½ inch deep of cucumber pulp and discard. Arrange the cups in a serving platter.

Combine the crab meat, cilantro, tomato, and onions in a mixing bowl. Add the mashed avocado and the mayonnaise, and toss well to combine the ingredients and flavors. Adjust the seasoning by adding salt & pepper as needed.

TO ASSEMBLE:

Top the cucumber cups generously with the crab salad and finish the dish by sprinkling them with minced parsley.

MAIN DISHES

MAIN DISHES

for Arturo and Verónica
"disfruta, come y bebe que la vida es breve" –dicho mexicano

FILET MIGNON IN PEPPERCORN SAUCE

FILETE MIGNON A LA PIMIENTA VERDE

Serves 6

Ingredients:
6 beef tenderloin medallions, 6 oz each
3 tablespoons of butter
Salt & pepper to taste

Ingredients for the peppercorn sauce:
1/2 cup of Brandy
1 oz of canned green peppercorns
4 cups of demi-glace or beef stock
2 cups fresh cream or whipping cream
1 1/2 tablespoon of Dijon mustard
3 tablespoons of butter
Salt & pepper to taste

TO PREPARE:

Preheat oven to 350°F.

Sprinkle the medallions with salt and pepper. Heat the butter in a skillet until very hot. Sear them for 2 minutes on each side and place them in the oven. Baking times will vary depending on how well you want the meats done: For rare bake 6 minutes, for medium-rare bake 8 minutes, for medium bake for 12 minutes, and for well done bake for 16+ minutes.

Meanwhile, prepare the peppercorn sauce in the same skillet and butter you seared the meats in.

TO PREPARE THE PEPPERCORN SAUCE:

Add the peppercorns to the pan and mash them coarsely with a fork. Add ½ an ounce of the green peppercorn juice and stir lightly. Add the brandy and flame it. Then, add the demi-glace or beef stock and stir again to incorporate well. Allow the mixture to simmer over low heat and for it to reduce to about 3 cups. When done, it should have a light sauce consistency. Then, add the fresh cream or whipping cream and bring it to a boil and stir all the time until sauce begins to thicken. Lastly, season the sauce with the Dijon mustard and bring the sauce together with the butter, while whisking constantly. Adjust the seasoning with salt and pepper if needed.

Drizzle the sauce over the beef medallions and serve immediately.

FILET TIPS SAUTÉED IN ANCHO-PASILLA SAUCE

PUNTAS DE FILETE EN SALSA DE CHILES ANCHOS Y PASILLA

Serves 4

Ingredients:

2.2 lbs of filet tips
3 ancho chiles, seeded and membranes removed
3 pasilla chiles, seeded and membranes removed
2 garlic cloves
1/4 cup of olive oil
1 cup of heavy whipping cream
1/2 cup of cilantro
1 packet of chicken bouillon
Sesame seeds, as needed
Salt & pepper to taste

TO PREPARE THE ANCHO-PASILLA SALSA:

Warm the olive oil in a large frying pan over medium-high heat and add the cleaned chiles, garlic cloves and the cilantro. Stir and cook for 3 minutes, reduce the heat to medium-low, and cook for an additional 2 minutes. Transfer the contents including the oil into the blender jar and mix on high while adding the whipping cream slowly in a thin stream, until everything is well blended. Set aside.

Salt and pepper the filet tips and fry them in the same pan that the chiles were cooked in. As soon as the meat begins to brown, add the ancho-pasilla sauce and continue cooking, occasionally stirring, until the filet tips are well cooked.

TO SERVE:

Transfer to a deep serving platter and sprinkle with sesame seeds. Serve alongside rice and accompany with warm corn tortillas.

PORK TENDERLOIN IN SWEET RED WINE AND ROASTED GARLIC SAUCE

LOMO DE PUERCO EN SALSA DULCE DE VINO ROJO Y AJO ROSTIZADO

Serves 6

Ingredients:
1 pork tenderloin
3 tablespoons of butter
Salt & pepper to taste

Ingredients for the red wine and sweet roasted garlic sauce:
4 garlic cloves with skin, roasted
1 cup of brown sugar
2 cups of red wine, preferably a Merlot (personal choice)

TO PREPARE:

Preheat oven to 350°F.

Salt and pepper the pork tenderloin and sear it in the hot butter. Transfer the tenderloin to a baking pan and put it in the oven.

Meanwhile, roast the garlic, unpeeled, until the skins darken. Put the wine and the sugar in a small saucepan over medium heat, stirring occasionally until it reduces to half its volume and somewhat thickens. Once the wine sauce has reduced, transfer it to the blender jar, add the peeled roasted garlic cloves and blend until very smooth.

Pour and baste the tenderloin with 1/2 of the red wine sauce while it continues to bake. Constantly check the tenderloin for doneness. The pork will be cooked when the center is slightly pink.

Remove it from the oven and let stand for 5 minutes. Slice the tenderloin and pour the remaining of the sauce over it. Serve immediately.

CHICKEN MEDALLIONS IN ASSORTED MUSHROOM AND CHIPOTLE SAUCE

MEDALLONES DE POLLO EN SALSA DE HONGOS Y CHIPOTLE

Serves 6

Ingredients for the chicken:
1 whole chicken, any size, completely thawed
Butcher string
Paprika, as needed
Salt & pepper to taste

Ingredients for the assorted mushroom chipotle sauce:
16 oz assorted mushrooms, coarsely chopped
1 small onion, chopped
1 garlic clove, minced
1 small can of chipotle chiles in their sauce
1 1/2 cups of heavy cream
1/2 cup of cilantro, finely chopped
1 tablespoon of butter
1 packet of chicken bouillon
Salt and coarse pepper to taste

TO PREPARE:

Preheat oven to 400°F.

Skin the chicken carefully starting with a slit at the chest area, as if you were taking off a coat and cut/peel it off carefully; *the skin needs to be practically intact for the recipe to work.* Set the skin aside. Cut the rest of the chicken meat into uneven chunk. Throw the bones out or save them to make chicken stock.

Lay the skin out flat and smooth on a clean workable area. Place the pieces of chicken meat randomly on top of the skin and when all the pieces are in it, salt them very lightly, sprinkle with paprika and wrap the chicken pieces tightly in the skin. It should look like a cylinder or a rocket. Tie with butcher string to hold it together in place. Lightly salt and pepper the skin and rub it in well.

Heat a skillet over medium-high heat and place the chicken cylinder on it. Sear on all sides until the skin is slightly crunchy and brown and transfer it to a baking pan. Bake for 20 minutes before checking for doneness. If not thoroughly cooked when you check it, turn it over on other side and bake for another 15 minutes before checking it again. Once the chicken is fully cooked, transfer it to a serving platter. Undo the butcher's string carefully and let stand for 5 minutes before slicing it.

While the chicken is baking, prepare the sauce.

TO PREPARE THE SAUCE:

Melt the butter in a large frying pan over medium heat. Add the chopped onions and garlic. Let cook until the onions become translucent. Add the mushrooms and cook them until they shrink and reduce in size while constantly stirring to prevent them from burning. Add the packet of chicken bouillon and the heavy cream. Keep stirring to incorporate everything. Lastly add the chopped cilantro, 1 full chipotle chile from the can plus two tablespoons of the chipotle sauce, and mix well. The sauce will be ready when all the liquid has been evaporated and is replaced with a creamy, glossy consistency.

TO SERVE:

Slice the chicken into ½-inch medallions, arrange them on the serving platter and pour the mushroom sauce evenly over them.

Alternatively, you can prepare boneless chicken breasts with the sauce if you don't have the time to prepare the medallions.

CHICKEN IN FIG AND RED WINE SAUCE

POLLO EN SALSA DE HIGOS Y VINO ROJO

Serves 6

Ingredients:
12 assorted pieces of chicken, skinless (breasts, thighs, drumsticks)
Allspice
Olive oil
Salt & pepper to taste

Ingredients for the fig and red wine sauce:
3 cups of red wine
10 figs, cut in small pieces
1 small shallot
1/2 cup of brown sugar
1/8 teaspoon of powdered cloves
1 tablespoon of red wine vinegar
1 tablespoon of butter

TO PREPARE THE CHICKEN:

Preheat oven to 350°F.

Arrange the chicken pieces on a baking sheet and rub them with the olive oil, salt, pepper, and a pinch of allspice. *Make sure to go very light on the allspice or it may overpower the dish.* Bake the chicken until well cooked but still moist.

TO PREPARE THE SAUCE:

Meanwhile, in a medium sized saucepan, melt the butter, add the finely chopped shallots and cook until caramelized. When the shallots turn translucent and soft, add the red wine, the vinegar, the figs, the powdered cloves, brown sugar, and bring to a boil over medium-high heat. Once it comes to a boil, reduce heat to medium-low and allow it to reduce and thicken slightly, while constantly stirring, for about 10 minutes. Remove it from the heat and transfer to the blender jar. Allow it to cool for about 5 minutes and then blend until a smooth sauce is achieved. Return it to the saucepan and reheat on low for another 5 minutes.

TO SERVE:

Transfer the chicken pieces to a serving platter and pour the sauce on top evenly making sure they are fully coated. Also, if some of the sauce is left over, put it in a gravy plate for extra servings.

PIBIL CHICKEN
POLLO PIBIL

Serves 6

Ingredients:
6 chicken breasts, boneless & skinless
Banana leaves (found in the freezer section), cut to size
1 red ripe tomato, cut into thin slices
6 serrano or jalapeño chiles
1 red onion, cut into very thin slices

Ingredients for the marinade:
3 bitter oranges, juiced
2 big green limes, juiced
2 garlic cloves, minced
12 peppercorns
Oregano, as desired
Paprika, as desired
Achiote sazón, 1 packet
Sea salt, as desired

Ingredients for the paste:
1 cup of achiote paste
1 garlic clove
2 tablespoons of paprika
1/8 teaspoon of cumin
Oregano
Sea salt & pepper to taste

TO PREPARE:

★The day before: Put all of the ingredients of the marinade in a big Tupperware or in a giant zip-lock bag. Put the chicken breasts in it and let sit overnight in the refrigerator. Shake them every time you get the chance.

On the day of serving, preheat oven to 350°F. Prepare the paste by mixing the achiote paste, garlic, paprika, cumin, oregano, sea salt, and pepper.

Place each chicken breast in the middle of a banana leaf, rub with the paste, and top each one with a couple of thin slices of onion, 1 slice of tomato and half of the chile serrano. Wrap the chicken breast by closing and folding the leaf to resemble a pocket and bake them. Check every 20 minutes until the chicken is fully cooked

CHICKEN PIECES IN CILANTRO CREAMY SAUCE

TROZOS DE POLLO EN SALSA CREMOSA DE CILANTRO

Serves 8-10

Ingredients for the chicken:
10 Chicken Breasts or Tenderloins, thawed and cut into 1-inch pieces
Olive oil, as needed
Allspice, a pinch
Salt & Pepper to taste

Ingredients for the cilantro sauce:
1 cup of cilantro, chopped
4 garlic cloves, peeled
1 packet of chicken bouillon
2 cups of heavy whipping cream
Salt & pepper to taste

TO PREPARE THE CREAMY CILANTRO SAUCE:

Put all of the sauce ingredients in the blender jar and mix until well incorporated. Taste and adjust the seasoning with salt & pepper if needed. If the mixture is too thick you can add 1 oz of water or chicken broth to release the blades.

TO PREPARE THE CHICKEN:

Once the creamy cilantro sauce has been prepared, heat the olive oil in a frying pan over medium heat. Fry the chicken pieces, stirring constantly, until almost done. Add the creamy cilantro sauce and finish cooking the chicken in the sauce.

TO SERVE:

Serve with a leafy green salad, rice, and accompany with tortillas and salsas.

CHICKEN AND HAM PATTIES

CROQUETAS DE POLLO Y JAMÓN

Serves 4

Ingredients:
2 chicken breasts
12 ham slices
4 eggs
6 tablespoons of flour
2 cups of milk
2 tablespoons of onion, minced
2 tablespoons of parsley, minced
1 tablespoon of mustard
Bread crumbs, as needed
Vegetable oil, enough to fry
1 avocado, sliced (optional)
1 tomato, sliced (optional)
Salt & pepper to taste

TO PREPARE:

Cook the chicken breasts in boiling water.

Chop the cooked chicken breasts and the ham into very small pieces and mix them together. Set aside.

Fry the onion in 2 tablespoons of vegetable oil and slowly add the flour. When the flour begins to brown, add the milk and cook for 10 more minutes, while all the time stirring. Add the chicken and the ham, the mustard and parsley, season with salt and pepper and cook until it turns into a thick paste. Set aside to cool.

Heat enough vegetable oil to fry the patties. Meanwhile, beat the eggs. When the oil is hot, form the patties, coat them with the egg and cover them completely with the bread crumbs. Fry the patties on both sides until well cooked.

Serve with avocado and tomato slices

ZUCCHINI, CORN AND CHEESE CRÊPES

CREPAS RELLENAS DE CALABACITAS, ELOTES Y QUESO

Serves 6

Ingredients for the crêpes:
3 cups of milk
6 eggs
2/3 cups of flour
8 tablespoons of butter, melted
1 tablespoons of dry thyme
1/8 of a teaspoon of salt
Additional butter if you don't have a non-stick pan

Ingredients for the filling:
2 cups of Monterey Jack cheese
1 cups of mild Cheddar cheese
1 cup of zucchini, finely chopped
1/2 cup of corn kernels
1/2 cup of fresh cilantro, finely chopped or minced
1/2 cup of red or white onion, very finely chopped
1 tablespoon of butter

TO PREPARE THE CRÊPES:

Preheat oven at 350°F.

Put the milk and eggs in a bowl and mix well with a whisk. Add the flour a little at a time and keep mixing until well combined. Add the melted butter, thyme, salt, and whisk well.

Prepare a plate with paper towels. Heat a pan (preferably a non-stick) over medium heat. Once heated, reduce the heat to medium low. *If the pan is not non-stick you will need a bit of butter to prevent the crêpes from sticking and breaking.* Pour ¼ cup of batter into the pan. Immediately grab the pan by the handle and remove it from the heat making circling

motions so as to cover the bottom of the pan with the crêpe batter. Return the pan to the heat and continue cooking until the edges of the crêpe begin to dry and the center is set, usually about 30 seconds. Use a spatula to flip it over to the other side and cook for an additional 8-10 seconds. Slide the crêpe onto a plate covered with paper towels. Repeat the process until all the crêpe batter has been used. Cover the crêpes with a paper towel and set aside while you prepare the filling.

TO PREPARE THE FILLING:

Sauté the vegetables in the butter until cooked and set aside. Mix both cheeses together in a bowl and set aside.

TO ASSEMBLE:

Fill the crêpes with the vegetables and the cheese down the middle, roll them up like a taco and place them in a baking dish. Bake the stuffed crêpes for about 20 minutes or so, until the cheese inside has completely melted. Serve immediately.

GARLIC SHRIMP

CAMARONES AL AJILLO

Serves 8-10

Ingredients:

20 jumbo shrimp, rinsed, uncooked, shells intact

3/4 cup of olive oil, separated

1 large white onion, cut in half

4 large garlic cloves, whole

1 teaspoon of fine sea salt

1/2 teaspoon of ground black pepper

TO PREPARE:

Purée 1/2 cup of the olive oil, the onion, garlic, salt, and pepper in the blender. Place the shrimp in a mixing bowl, stir in the puréed mixture and marinate it for 1 hour in the refrigerator.

Heat the remaining ¼ cup of the olive oil in a large frying pan over medium-high heat. Add the shrimp with all of the marinade and sauté just until the shrimp are opaque in the center and cooked, about 5 to 6 minutes. Serve immediately.

BEEF FILETS IN AVOCADO TEQUILA-LIME SAUCE

FILETE EN SALSA DE AGUACATE AL TEQUILA Y LIMÓN

Serves 6

Ingredients:
6 beef filets
2 tablespoons of olive oil
Salt & pepper to taste

Ingredients for the Avocado Tequila-Lime Sauce:
2 avocados, mashed
2 tablespoons of cilantro, minced
2 tablespoons of parsley, minced
2 tablespoons of freshly squeezed lime juice
2 oz of tequila
1/2 tablespoon of coarse sea or kosher salt
Pepper to taste
6 cherry tomatoes (optional)

TO PREPARE:

Lightly salt and pepper the filets and fry them in olive oil until cooked as desired. For well done filets, you may want to butterfly them open.

TO PREPARE THE SAUCE:

Mince the parsley and the cilantro. Mash the avocado with the salt to a smooth paste. Add the 2 tablespoons of lime juice, the parsley and cilantro and mix well. Lastly, add the tequila and stir to incorporate well. Adjust the seasoning by adding more salt and pepper if needed.

TO SERVE:

Arrange the filets on a serving platter or plate them individually. Top each one with a generous scoop of the avocado tequila-lime sauce. Place a cherry tomato in the middle of each filet for decoration.

SEAFOOD MEDLEY SHELLS BAKED IN A BUTTER, GARLIC AND BACON SAUCE

CONCHAS DE MARISCOS HORNEADAS EN SALSA DE MANTEQUILLA, AJO Y TOCINO

Serves 6

Ingredients:

6 large flat ceramic shells
1 cup of small shrimp, cooked without a tail
1 cup of oysters, fresh
1 cup of scallops, fresh, chopped
1 – 8 oz butter stick, softened
6 garlic cloves, minced
1/2 cup of cilantro or parsley, minced
3 limes, halved (optional)
4 slices of bacon, cooked and crumbled
1/2 cup of bread crumbs
Coarse sea salt & pepper, freshly ground

TO PREPARE:

Preheat oven to 375°F.

Put the crumbled bacon, the softened butter and the minced garlic in a bowl. Mix them well with a hand-held mixer until the butter is light and fluffy. Set aside.

Put the chopped shrimp, scallops and oysters in a mixing bowl, sprinkle them lightly with the sea salt and freshly ground pepper and mix well to incorporate.

Line a baking sheet with the ceramic shells and stuff them with the seafood medley, about ½ a cup each. Spoon 2 generous tablespoons of the butter mixture on top of each shell and sprinkle with some bread crumbs and minced fresh cilantro or parsley. Bake for about 10 to 20 minutes, depending on your oven. Check regularly for doneness. The shells will be done when all the butter mixture has melted, is boiling lightly and the breadcrumbs begin to brown. Remove them from the oven and serve immediately. Be careful to not over bake.

TO SERVE:

Arrange each shell in an individual plate with a lime half. You can also enjoy this dish accompanied with saltine crackers and a simple tomato and avocado salad.

SWEET DELICACIES
AND DESSERTS

SWEET DELICACIES AND DESSERTS

for Patrick, my son
"con azúcar y miel hasta los caracoles saben bien" –dicho mexicano

During colonial times in the 17th century, convents played a major role in the development of the neo-Hispanic cuisines. These were the times when European and Asian spices and food items were being introduced to the New World and the convent nuns were given the freedom and encouragement to develop new recipes using what they had available. The nuns -most likely guided by their sweets patron saint San Pascual Baylón - were then able to skillfully combine the indigenous and European ingredients creating new delicacies and eating habits while at the same time, making convent kitchens the birthplace of traditional jellies, candies, desserts, moles, and the world renowned sweet and slightly-alcoholic beverage: eggnog.

Sor Juana Inés de la Cruz was such a nun. Her face is currently embossed on the Mexican $200 pesos currency bills but, back then, she was a highly controversial woman within the Catholic Church. Sor Juana had a great talent for writing, a medium she used frequently and freely to speak her mind and render her opinions. She mainly wrote poetry and theater plays in a baroque style that was very hard to read and understand; but nonetheless, her works were, and still are, very well liked and it is what gained her the title of the tenth muse. However, little is known about the recipe books and food chronicles she transcribed and wrote about; they have become very hard to access. But it is known she had a great love for food, in particular for desserts and candies as she clearly states this in her sonnets. Through researching her life and work, I came across a few recipes and was spellbound by the names the nuns had chosen to give certain dishes: *heavenly torte*, *table-cover blemish*, *this-tastes-so-good*, etc. Some of these recipes are still enjoyed by Mexicans today but regrettably, with a slightly different name attached to them.

Fruits have always been essential to the cuisines of Mexico. They are used to make juices and fresh waters;

they are the basic ingredients in certain candies such as *ate* –a fruit paste- and *camotes* –starchy candies made primarily with sweet potatoes or yams, as they are in jellies and preserves. Depending on the case, we begin our meals with fruit cocktails or end them with fruit salads. Individual fruit pieces are highly regarded as standalone desserts and they are also used in the confection of pies and simple cakes. Honey, corn, beans, seeds, spices, and cacao that have been used to make sweet treats since pre-Hispanic times, are just as important as fruits in the dessert and candy confectioning realm. Without a doubt, these simple desserts and candies will surprise and invigorate your senses.

PECAN CRÈME

CREMA DE NUEZ

Serves 6

Ingredients:
1 tablespoon of butter
3 cups of milk
2 cinnamon sticks
3/4 cup of granulated sugar, separated
2 tablespoons of cornstarch
2 1/4 cups of pecans, roughly chopped, plus a few whole for decoration
2 egg yolks
1/3 cup of brandy or rum
10 lady fingers

TO PREPARE:

Lightly butter a shallow glass Pyrex. Set aside.

Grind the nuts with 2 tablespoons of the sugar. Set aside until ready to use.

Bring the milk to a soft boil. Add the cinnamon and stir in the rest of the sugar. Lower the heat and continue stirring until the sugar is completely dissolved. Transfer ¼ of a cup of the warmed milk-sugar mixture into the cornstarch and work it to a smooth paste. Stir this paste back into the milk-sugar mixture and continue cooking over low heat, stirring all the time, until it thickens slightly.

Add the ground pecans to the milk mixture. Cook it until it has reduced and thickened for an additional 20 to 30 minutes. Then, transfer ½ cup of the milk mixture to the egg yolks and beat well. Return this egg mixture to the milk and continue to cook, stirring and scraping the bottom of the pan to prevent it from burning and sticking. *Once this mixture is creamy and thick, it should cover a wooden spoon thickly, add the brandy or rum and continue to stir.*

TO ASSEMBLE:

Pour half of the pecan crème into the lightly buttered glass dish. Cover with the lady fingers, and then pour the remaining pecan crème over the lady fingers. Decorate the top with the whole nuts and set aside to cool at room temperature. Do not refrigerate before serving. It can be stored in the refrigerator, covered, but always serve it at room temperature.

CREAM CUSTARD WITH MILK CARAMEL

NATILLA DE CAJETA

Serves 6

Ingredients:
1 can (12 oz) of evaporated milk
1 can (12 oz) of water
1 cup of cajeta (recipe found on page 208) alternatively, use Dulce de Leche
4 egg yolks
2 tablespoons of cornstarch, diluted in 2 tablespoons of water
4 tablespoons of butter
Sugar, as needed
Blackberries, to garnish (optional)

TO PREPARE:

Dilute the cornstarch in 2 tablespoons of water. Set aside.

Mix the milk, the water and cajeta in a saucepan over medium heat, while stirring constantly. When it begins to boil, add the diluted cornstarch and the egg yolks, continuing to stir to incorporate well.

The *natilla* will be ready when it thickens to the consistency of a pudding. Immediately remove it from the heat and add the butter mixing well to fully incorporate.

TO ASSEMBLE:

Pour the *natilla* into 6 individual ceramic ramekins. Sprinkle each one lightly but evenly with sugar and flame them with a kitchen torch to caramelize the sugar. Top each one with a couple of blackberries.

BURNT MILK WITH PRUNE COMPOTE

LECHE QUEMADA CON COMPOTA DE CIRUELA

Serves 6

Ingredients for the burnt milk:
4 cups of whipping cream
1 vanilla stick
cup of sugar
8 egg yolks

Ingredients for the compote:
2 tablespoons of butter
3 tablespoons of sugar
1 cup of orange juice
lb of prunes, diced in very small pieces

TO PREPARE THE COMPOTE:

Melt the butter over medium heat. Add the sugar and the orange juice. Bring it to a boil until the mixture becomes thicker, for about two minutes. Add the prunes to the mixture and mix well. Reduce the heat to low and allow it to cook for 10 more minutes. Stir to prevent it from burning. Refrigerate until ready to assemble the dessert.

TO PREPARE THE BURNT MILK:

Heat the whipping cream and the vanilla stick in a saucepan just until it begins to boil. Remove from heat and set aside.

Beat the egg yolks with the sugar until light and fluffy and the sugar is completely incorporated. Remove the vanilla stick from the hot whipping cream and then pour it into the egg yolk mixture in a fine stream while vigorously whisking by hand, to prevent the egg yolks from cooking.

Return it to the stove over low heat for 10 more minutes, continuing to whisk constantly. Remove from heat and allow the mixture to cool while whisking vigorously, for about 5 more minutes.

Pour into molds and refrigerate over night. Before serving, sprinkle some additional sugar on top of the burnt milk and flame it to caramelize.

TO SERVE:

Place a generous spoonful of compote on top or on the side of the burnt milk. The burnt milk should be served at room temperature, and the compote should be served warm.

BANANA CRÊPES WITH MEXICAN CHOCOLATE SAUCE

CREPAS DE PLÁTANO CON SALSA DE CHOCOLATE MEXICANO

Makes 14-15 Crêpes

Ingredients for the crêpes:
1 1/2 cups of milk
3 eggs
1-1/3 cups of flour
4 tablespoons of butter, melted
1 tablespoon of bitter orange zest, grated
Additional butter to cook the crêpes, as needed

Ingredients for the banana filling:
2 bananas
2 tablespoons of butter
2 tablespoons of sugar
1 oz of rum

Ingredients for the Mexican chocolate sauce:
1 can of evaporated milk
2 Mexican chocolate tablets (Abuelita)
1 tablespoon of butter
2 tablespoons of corn starch, diluted in 2 tablespoons of cold water

TO PREPARE THE CRÊPES:

Put the milk, the orange zest and the eggs in a bowl and mix them well with a balloon whisk. Add the flour a little at a time and keep mixing until well incorporated. Melt the butter and add it to the mixture while whisking to fully integrate all of the ingredients.

Cover a plate with paper towels. Heat a frying pan (preferably a non-stick) over medium heat and once heated, reduce to medium-low. *If the frying pan is not non-stick you will need a bit of butter to prevent the crêpes from sticking and breaking.* Pour about 1/4 of a cup of mixture into the frying pan, and grabbing the pan by the handle, remove it from the stove and make circling motions to ensure the batter covers the whole bottom of the pan. Return the pan to the stove to continue cooking the crêpe. Once the edges look cooked and the center is set, using a spatula, turn the crêpe over and leave and additional 10 seconds on the reverse side. Slide the crêpe off onto the paper towels. Repeat the process until all of the crêpe mixture has been used. Cover the crêpes with a paper towel and set aside while you prepare the filling

TO PREPARE THE BANANA FILLING:

Cut the bananas into little cubes. In a small skillet, melt the butter over medium heat and add the banana cubes. Toss and sprinkle them with sugar. Add the rum, remove from heat and flame the bananas. Return to the stovetop once the flame has consumed. Toss the bananas once again and set aside until ready to use.

TO PREPARE THE MEXICAN CHOCOLATE SAUCE:

In small saucepan over medium heat, bring the evaporated milk to a simmer. Remove from heat and add the 2 tablets of Mexican chocolate. Let them rest for a moment, undisturbed, so as to soften the tablets and then with a small whisk finish breaking up the chocolate. Whisk well until the chocolate mixture is smooth and even. Return it to the stove over low heat and continue whisking. Dilute the cornstarch in 2 tablespoons of water and mix well until smooth. Take 1 tablespoon of the diluted corn starch and add it to the chocolate sauce. Mix gently and then add a second tablespoon of diluted corns tarch into the chocolate sauce. Mix well again and when the sauce is smooth and begins to thicken, remove it from the heat. Lastly, add the butter and stir well to bring the sauce together. Set aside.

TO ASSEMBLE:

Fill one crêpe at a time. Take a small spoonful of banana filling and spread it in the middle of the crêpe. Close the crêpes by folding them in half and then in half again, forming a triangle. Repeat until all crêpes are filled.

TO SERVE:

Arrange the stuffed crêpes either on a dessert serving platter or on individual plates and cover the crêpes generously with the chocolate sauce. Serve immediately.

LIME DESSERT

POSTRE DE LIMÓN

Serves 8-10

This is a very simple and delicious dessert. Its tangy flavor and light consistency makes it a perfect ending to any meal.

Ingredients:
1 can (14 oz) of condensed milk
1 can (12 oz) of evaporated milk
7 small key-limes or 4 limes
The zest of two limes
15 María cookies or graham crackers
4 tablespoons of butter, melted

TO PREPARE THE COOKIE CRUST:

Preheat oven to 350°F.

Crush the María cookies and add the melted butter to the crumbs to form a paste. Press the cookie paste down, covering the bottom of a round, oven safe pie dish. *If you want the paste to go up the sides of the pie dish, simply prepare more of the cookie mixture.*

Bake for about 8-10 minutes or until the cookie crust has lightly browned and hardened. Remove it from the oven and allow it to cool completely at room temperature before adding the filling.

TO PREPARE THE FILLING:

While the cookie crust is cooling, zest the skin of 2 limes and set aside. Squeeze all of the limes to obtain their juice and then set aside.

Mix the evaporated milk and the condensed milk very well in the blender and then add the lime juice very slowly in a fine stream while still blending until well incorporated.

TO ASSEMBLE:

Pour the lime mixture onto the baked and cooled cookie crust, sprinkle it with the lime zest, and immediately transfer it to the refrigerator to set, uncovered. It is best to keep it in the refrigerator over night and to take it out just before serving.

*Alternatively, a good variation to this is dessert is to freeze it over night for a more ice-cream like dessert.

STRAWBERRY WRAPPED BABY

NIÑO ENVUELTO DE FRESA

Serves 8

InIngredients for the cake:
8 eggs, separated
1 1/2 cups of flour
1 1/2 cups of sugar
1 1/2 sticks of butter
3 teaspoons of baking powder
2 teaspoons of vanilla extract
Lemon zest

Ingredients for the filling:
2 cups of fresh strawberries, cut in small pieces
2 packages of cream cheese
1 cup of confectioners' sugar
1 cup of sour cream

TO PREPARE THE CAKE:

Preheat oven to 350°F.

In a large mixing bowl, beat the butter, the sugar, the 8 egg yolks, the flour, the baking powder, the lemon zest, and the vanilla extract until well incorporated and set aside.

In another bowl, *preferably stainless steel, very clean and dry or the egg whites might not fluff*, beat the eggs whites until they form stiff peaks.

Add the egg yolk mixture by folding gently, as if wrapping them together from the bottom to the top, until well incorporated.

Prepare the baking sheet by covering it with tin foil or parchment paper and then greasing and flouring it. Transfer the cake batter onto the baking sheet carefully and bake it for 12 to 15 minutes *baking time will depend on your oven*. When the cake is done, it will have a golden yellow hue and it will look spongy.

TO PREPARE THE FILLING:

While the cake is baking, beat the cream cheese and once soft, add the sour cream and keep beating until smooth. Then add the confectioners' sugar and continue to beat until well mixed and soft. Set aside.

TO ASSEMBLE:

You will need to work at a fast and steady pace because the more the cake cools, the more difficult it becomes to handle. Wet a clean, large dish cloth, ring out the excess water well and turn the cake over onto the cloth. Peel off any tin foil or wax paper residue carefully so as to not break the cake. Spread out the cream cheese filling smoothly throughout the whole cake, add the strawberry pieces and immediately start rolling the cake tightly using the dishcloth to help wrap it. Put it in the refrigerator until ready to eat. If there is enough cream filling and strawberries left over, use them to decorate the top of the cake. For an added visual impact, if you have some additional confectioners' sugar, you can sift a small amount on top of the cake before serving.

Alternatively, the cake can be filled with mangoes, peaches, pineapple or with ice-cream (see recipes for ice-cream beginning on page 188) and stored in the freezer, covered, after being rolled.

MARGARITA MOUSSE

MOUSSE DE MARGARITA

Serves 8

Ingredients:
1 packet of unflavored gelatin
1 cup of white sugar, separated
4 eggs, separated
3 tablespoons of lime juice
Zest of 1 lime
2 tablespoons of water
1/2 cup of white tequila
1/4 cup of triple sec
Pinch of salt

TO PREPARE:

Combine the gelatin, ½ a cup of the sugar and the salt in a glass saucepan. Set aside.

Beat the egg yolks until they are thick and creamy with an electric mixer. Add the lime juice, the water and continue mixing. Pour it into the saucepan containing the gelatin mixture and put the saucepan over medium heat for approximately 5 minutes mixing constantly. Whisk vigorously, but carefully, to avoid the egg yolks from cooking and for the gelatin to completely dissolve. The mixture should be smooth. *Please note that if the gelatin does not completely dissolve, the mousse will have a grainy texture.*

Remove from heat and add the tequila, triple sec and the grated lime zest, whisking all the time. Refrigerate and let cool.

While the egg mixture is cooling in the refrigerator, beat the egg whites, gradually incorporating the remaining sugar until they form stiff peaks.

Fold the egg yolk mixture gently into the egg whites until well incorporated. Fill the margarita or large wine glasses with about ½ a cup of the mousse mixture. Chill the mousse for at least 2 hours or until it sets, before serving.

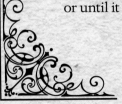

TO SERVE:

For an added visual impact, once the mousse is set, you can coat the glass rims with colored or white sugar.

YAM CANDY BARS FROM PUEBLA

CAMOTE DE PUEBLA

Ingredients:
2.2 lbs of sweet potatoes or yams
2.2 lbs of white sugar
1 cup superfine white sugar
1 1/2 cups of water
5 droplets of lime or orange essence
Zest of 1 lime
2 droplets of green, orange or yellow food coloring (optional)

TO PREPARE:

Cook the sweet potatoes or yams in boiling water until soft. Peel them completely and mash them until you form a paste. Set aside.

Dissolve the sugar in the water over medium-low heat, add the lime zest and stir continuously until a smooth and thick syrup is achieved. Remove from heat and spoon out any foam that might have formed during the process. Add the syrup to the sweet potato or yam paste and mix well to incorporate.

Strain the yam purée back into the saucepan and bring it to a boil over medium heat while all the time stirring with a wooden spoon and scraping the bottom of the saucepan to prevent from burning. Cook this mixture until it turns very thick and somewhat sticky. Remove from heat and allow it to cool just a bit. Add the essence and the food coloring if you are using any, and mix well to combine color and flavors.

Pour and extend the paste on a flat surface dish and allow it to cool and dry at room temperature.

TO ASSEMBLE:

Grab two generous tablespoons of the yam paste and roll it into a ball. Gently press it between your hands in a back and forth motion to slightly extend the paste to give it the shape of a thick and stubby cigar. Roll lightly in the superfine sugar coating the *camote* piece entirely and set aside on a cookie rack to dry completely. Once dry, if desired, carefully wrap the individual camote pieces in clear or colorful cellophane or wax paper and tie both ends with a ribbon.

MEXICAN WEDDING CAKES

POLVORONES

Makes about 4 dozen

Ingredients:

8 oz of butter at room temperature
2 teaspoons of vanilla extract
2 cups of all purpose flour
1 cup of almonds, coarsely ground
2 cups of powdered sugar, separated
1/8 teaspoon of powdered cinnamon

TO PREPARE:

Preheat oven to 350°F.

Beat the butter in a large bowl with an electric mixer until light and fluffy. Add ½ a cup of the powdered sugar and vanilla extract while still mixing. Add the flour and the almonds and continue to mix only until ingredients are incorporated; don't over mix. Divide the dough in half and make into two balls. Wrap them separately in plastic and refrigerate them for at least 30 minutes.

Sift together the remaining 1 ½ cup of powdered sugar and the cinnamon together into a deep plate and set aside.

Working with only half of the chilled dough, take 2 teaspoonfuls of dough and roll it between your palms to make small balls. Arrange the small dough balls in a baking sheet spacing them a ½ inch apart. Bake the cookies until golden brown in the bottom and pale golden on the top for about 18 minutes. Cool the cookies on a baking sheet for 5 minutes. Gently toss the warm cookies in the powdered sugar and cinnamon mixture to coat them completely. Repeat the procedure with the remaining dough. Sprinkle the remaining sugar on top of the cookies and serve.

They can be prepared two days ahead and stored in an airtight container at room temperature.

THREE MILKS AND MILK CARAMEL JELL-O WITH KAHLÚA SAUCE

GELATINA DE TRES LECHES Y CAJETA
CON SALSA DE KAHLÚA

Serves 8

This recipe provides three desserts in one. You can prepare only the three milks jell-o, only the cajeta jell-o or both to create a layered pattern dessert.

Ingredients for the three milk jell-o:
2 cups of whole milk
2 cups of evaporated milk
1 can (14 oz) of condensed milk
3 packets of unflavored gelatin such as Knox
1/4 cup of cold milk to dilute the gelatin

Ingredients for the cajeta (milk caramel) jell-o:
2 cups of cajeta (recipe found on page 208)
2 cups of whole milk
2 cups of vanilla ice-cream
3 packets of unflavored gelatin such as Knox
1/4 cup of cold milk, to dilute the gelatin

Ingredients for the Kahlúa sauce:
1 can (12 oz) of evaporated milk
1 can (14 oz) of condensed milk
4 oz of Kahlúa
2 tablespoons of cornstarch, diluted in 2 tablespoon of water

TO PREPARE THE THREE MILKS JELL-O:

Prepare the three milks jell-o first.

Dilute the unflavored gelatin in the ¼ cup of cold milk. Set aside.

Combine all of the milks in a large saucepan over medium heat while constantly stirring. Bring to a soft boil and add the diluted unflavored gelatin. Continue to stir until the gelatin has completely dissolved and to prevent the milk from burning.

Remove from heat and pour into a jell-o mold or individual glass ramekins filling them only half-way. Put it in the refrigerator while you prepare the cajeta jell-o.

TO PREPARE THE CAJETA JELL-O:

Heat the milk in a large sauce pan over medium heat. Bring to a soft simmer and add the ice-cream. Stir constantly until all of the ice cream is melted. Add the cajeta and incorporate well. Next, add the diluted unflavored gelatin and stir until the gelatin is completely dissolved.

Remove from heat and allow it to cool down at room temperature.

When the three milk jell-o is lightly set, gently pour the lukewarm cajeta jell-o over it, filling the rest of the mold(s) and return it to the refrigerator until it fully sets.

Meanwhile, prepare the Kahlúa sauce.

TO PREPARE THE KAHLÚA SAUCE:

Dilute the cornstarch in the 2 tablespoons of water. Set aside.

Combine the evaporated and condensed milks in a saucepan over medium-low heat. Add the Kahlúa and bring to a simmer while stirring all the time. Add 1 tablespoon of the diluted cornstarch and continue stirring until the sauce begins to thicken a little. If after 3 minutes of cooking the sauce has not yet begun to thicken, add another tablespoon of the diluted cornstarch. When done, the sauce should be smooth and slightly thick.

TO SERVE:

Un-mold the jell-o onto a serving platter, pour some of the Kahlúa sauce over it or serve it on the side.

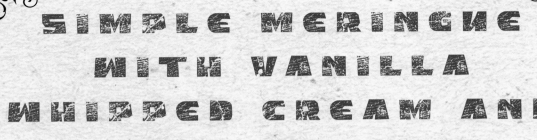

SIMPLE MERINGUE WITH VANILLA WHIPPED CREAM AND WILD BERRIES

MERENGUES CON CREMA BATIDA DE VAINILLA Y MORAS SILVESTRES

Serves 8

Ingredients for the meringues:
6 egg whites
1/4 teaspoon of cream of tartar
1 cup of sugar

Ingredients for the whipped cream and wild berries:
1 cup of assorted berries, chopped
1 cup of superfine sugar, separated
1 cup of whipping cream
6 droplets of vanilla extract

TO PREPARE THE MERINGUES:

Tip: To make sure the meringues turn out perfect, the recipe needs to be followed accurately. Also, your bowl and mixer blades must be very clean and dry, or the egg whites might not whip properly.

Preheat oven to 300°F.

Line 2 baking sheets with wax or baking paper. If you need to, draw 4-inch circles on the wax/baking paper to help guide you.

Begin by beating the egg whites with a handheld mixer, and slowly sprinkle the cream of tartar while all the time beating. When the egg whites turn white and foamy, gradually add the sugar and continue beating until stiff shiny peaks form. The entire process should take about four to five minutes.

Spoon the egg whites on to the baking sheets and create a circle pattern. Circles should be about 4 inches in diameter. Press the middle down with the back of the spoon and build up the edges slightly. Bake them until firm and dry for about 1 hour. Turn off the oven and open the door but do not remove the meringues or they will flatten. When the meringues are completely cool, remove them from the oven and peel off the wax/baking paper.

TO PREPARE THE VANILLA CREAM AND BERRIES:

While the meringues are cooling inside of the oven, chop the berries and sprinkle them with ½ a cup of sugar and set aside.

Beat the whipping cream and half way through the process add the remaining ½ cup of sugar gradually and the vanilla extract drops. Beat the whipping cream until it holds its shape.

TO ASSEMBLE:

Line the meringues on a serving platter and then scoop some of the whipping cream into each of their centers. Top them off with the chopped berries and the syrup they created. Serve immediately. *The meringues will get soggy with the cream filling and berries after a while, so make sure you only top as many meringues as you actually need or they might have to be thrown out.*

The meringue cups can be used immediately or they can be stored, uncovered, for a couple of days in a dry place without the filling. Don't refrigerate.

MILK AND PECAN CANDY

JAMONCILLO DE NUEZ

Ingredients:
2 cups of whole milk
4 cups (32 oz) of condensed milk
2 cups of pecans, chopped
1/3 cup of pecans, whole

TO PREPARE:

Combine the milks in a heavy saucepan and bring to a boil over medium heat. Cook while constantly stirring to prevent sticking and burning until the milk mixture has reduced, thickened, turned a slight pinkish-brown hue and you can clearly see the bottom of the saucepan.

Remove from heat and stir vigorously to cool.

TO ASSEMBLE:

Line a rectangular or square Pyrex with wax paper and pour half the mixture into it. Spread it out evenly and sprinkle the chopped pecans over the mixture. Pour the remaining mixture on top of the pecans and again spread it evenly throughout. Allow to cool and set at room temperature for 24 hours.

TO SERVE:

Un-mold onto a serving platter, remove the wax paper and decorate with the whole pecans. Cut into small square or rectangular pieces.

PINE NUT EGGNOG

ROMPOPE DE PIÑÓN

Ingredients:

2 cups of sugar

6 cups of milk

14 egg yolks

1 cup of rum

5 drops of vanilla extract

1 cup of pine nuts, finely ground

1 cinnamon stick

2 cloves, whole

TO PREPARE:

Put the cinnamon stick and cloves into the rum and allow the flavors to infuse for 24 hours.

Bring the milk and the sugar to a boil over medium heat in a heavy bottom saucepan. Add the ground pine nuts and the vanilla extract and continue to boil for 5 more minutes while all the time stirring to prevent it from burning. Remove from heat and set aside.

Beat the egg yolks until they form a ribbon and pour 1 cup of the boiled milk into them, whisking vigorously to prevent the egg yolks from cooking. Transfer the egg mixture into the saucepan with the boiled milk and cook it over low heat for an additional 10 minutes while all the time stirring.

Remove the cloves and the cinnamon from the rum and pour the rum into the eggnog. Mix well and allow it to cool at room temperature and then refrigerate. You can drink it cold, at room temperature or you can use it to prepare eggnog jell-o.

Alternatively, instead of pine nuts, you can use pecans, peanuts, almonds or pistachios

TRIPLE SEC FLAN WITH CARAMEL-ORANGE SAUCE

FLAN DE TRIPLE SEC CON SALSA DE CARAMELO Y NARANJA

Serves 6-8

Unlike more delicate flans, the ones that are made with condensed milk or cream cheese result richer in texture.

Ingredients for the flan:
1 can (14 oz) of condensed milk
1 can (12 oz) of evaporated milk
3 oz of white sugar
2 oz of triple sec
1 teaspoon of vanilla extract
6 eggs

Ingredients for the orange sauce:
2 cups of orange juice, freshly squeezed
1 cup of confectioners' sugar
1 tablespoon of butter
1 oz triple sec

TO PREPARE:

Preheat oven to 350°F.

Put the condensed milk, evaporated milk, triple sec, vanilla extract, and eggs in the blender jar. Mix the ingredients until completely incorporated. Set aside.

Melt the sugar in a saucepan over medium heat. *The sugar will melt very quickly; make sure you remove it from the heat before it burns or the taste of the flan will be bitter.*

Pour the melted sugar into a loaf pan, preferably glass, making sure it distributes evenly throughout the bottom of the pan. Pour in the flan mixture carefully to avoid indents in the melted sugar.

Put the loaf pan containing the flan mixture in a larger baking pan. Add enough water to come halfway up the sides of the loaf pan. Bake the flan in the water bath until it is set in the center for about 35 to 40 minutes. Check for doneness by inserting a toothpick or sharp knife towards the middle of the flan. If it comes out clean, the flan is done baking. If it does not, put it back in oven and check it frequently. Once it is done baking, remove it from the water bath and let it cool at room temperature. The flan will continue to firm up as it cools.

When you check the flan, if it still hasn't set but is developing a golden brown film on the top, don't be concerned. Focus on getting the flan to fully cook and then, after the flan cools, gently peel of the golden brown film before serving, it comes off very easily.

TO PREPARE THE ORANGE SAUCE:

Mix the orange juice, confectioners' sugar and triple sec in a saucepan and bring it to a boil over medium heat. Cook the sauce for 5 more minutes and then add the butter. Whisk vigorously for an additional minute and remove it from the heat.

TO SERVE:

Un-mold the flan directly onto a serving platter. Cut it into 1 ½ - inch slices and always serve at room temperature alongside the warm orange sauce.

G L O S S A R Y

Alfeñiques: Sugar based figurines that are confectioned over the Day of the Dead and Day of all Saints celebrations

Antojitos: Meaning *little cravings*, it refers to snacks

Atole: A drink made of maize

Calaveritas: Sugar skulls made of sugar or chocolate

Cantina: A drinking establishment

Cempazúchitl: Marigold; a very popular flower used during the day of the Dead and Day of all Saints celebrations

Charamusca: Sugar ribbon

Comal: A flat, round griddle used in Mexican cooking since pre-Hispanic times. Aztecs used them to cook over an open fire. Today, we use them to heat tortillas or roast vegetables or chiles

Copal: A fossilized resin that burns and produces an odor much like incense

Esperanto: A language not of any country or ethnic group, based on words common to all European languages

Estudiantina: A type of music band

Garnachas : Foods made by deep-frying maize dough; such as taquitos, sopes and quesadillas

Guajolote: Turkey

Horchata: Rice water

Huichol: An indigenous ethnic group from Mexico, and it also refers to their native language

Mariachis: A type of music group

Metate: A ground stone tool used for processing grain and seeds that has been used since pre-Hispanic times

Mojiganga: A parade of giant puppets

Molcajete: A mortar and pestle made of volcanic rock or basalt stone that has been used since pre-Hispanic times to grind and smash seeds, condiments and to make salsas

Mole: A traditional Mexican sauce made with chiles, chocolate and spices

Pan de Muerto: Bread of the Dead; a sweet bread prepared during the Day of the Dead and the Day of all Saints celebrations

Papel Picado: A traditional and colorful Mexican paper decoration

Pulque: A fermented fruit drink

Talavera: Mexican pottery

Tamales: A traditional type of indigenous Mexican food prepared with maize dough that is wrapped and cooked in corn husks

Tomatillo: A small green Mexican fruit from the family of the tomatoes, not to be confused with green tomatoes

Wirikuta: Meaning *the Sacred Path* in the Huichol language

RECIPE INDEX

**MEXICAN STAPLE APPETIZER DISHES &
SPECIAL OCCASIONS
LOS ANTOJITOS Y ENTREMESES MEXICANOS
& LAS OCASIONES ESPECIALES**

Bean Tamales
Tamales de Frijol...128

Black Mole Poblano with Chicken or Turkey
Mole Poblano con Pollo o Guajolote.....................118

Bread of the Dead
Pan de Muerto 110

Corn and Honey Tamales
Tamales de Elote con Miel.................................154

Drunken Beans
Frijoles Borrachos.. 260

Enchiladas Stuffed with Chicken and Cheese in
    Chile Poblano Sauce
*Enchiladas Rellenas de Pollo y Queso con Salsa de
    Chile Poblano* 138

Flora's Onion and Cilantro Dip
Dip de Cebolla y Cilantro Estilo Flora 49

Guacamole
Guacamole... 92

Melted Cheese with Chile Strips
Cazuelitas de Queso Fundido con Rajas de Chile .. 96

Miner-Style Enchiladas
Enchiladas Mineras de la Capital 178

Pot Beans
Frijoles de Olla..144

Ranchero-Style Eggs
Huevos Rancheros...136

Real Quesadillas
Quesadillas..116

Red Chilaquiles
Chilaquiles Rojos 140

Refried Beans
Frijoles Refritos..145

Sopecitos
Sopecitos.. 94

Sweet Tamales
Tamales Dulces..130

Swiss Enchiladas
Enchiladas Suizas 50

Tortillas Stuffed with Scrambled Eggs Baked in a
    Hearty Bean Sauce with Chorizo
*Enfrijoladas Rellenas de Huevos Revueltos con
    Chorizo* 142

Trio of Plain, Ham and Bacon Molletes
Trío de Molletes de Queso, Jamón y Tocino 180

BEVERAGES AND FRESH FRUIT WATERS
LAS AGUAS FRESCAS Y LAS BEBIDAS

Classic Shaken Margaritas
Margaritas Clásicas..97

Cucumber Water
Agua de Pepino 40

Guava Maize Drink
Atole de Guayaba...127

Hibiscus Flower Water
Agua de Jamaica 39

Mexican Clay Pot Coffee
Café de Olla 157

Mexican-Style Hot Chocolate
Chocolate Caliente 126

Michelada (beer drink)
Michelada... 98

Pine Nut Eggnog
Rompope de Piñón...............................311

Rice Water
Agua de Horchata 38

Watermelon Water
Agua de Sadía...41

SOUPS
LAS SOPAS

Bean Soup with Cactus
Sopa de Frijol con Nopalitos 68

Chicken Red Pozole
Pozole Rojo de Pollo..148

Mexican Style Vermicelli
Fideos al Horno...................................... 70

Mushroom and Zucchini Soup
Sopa de Hongos y Calabacitas 146

Tortilla Soup
Sopa de Tortilla 184

EUROPEAN SELECTIONS
LOS PLATILLOS EUROPEOS

Carrots and Prunes – Tzimes
Tzimes- Zanahorias con Ciruelas 29

Chicken in Sweet and Sour Apricot Sauce
Pollo en Salsa Agridulce de Chabacano 28

Chopped Liver
Higaditos Picados 20

Grandma Hanka's Egg Salad
Ensalada de Huevo de la Abuela Hanka............... 23

Herring Salad
Ensalada de Arenque.. 22

Sour Pickles
Pepinos Agrios 26

Sweet Purple Cabbage
Col Morada..27

Viennese Sausage and Potato Salad
Ensalada de Salchicha Vienesa y Papa 25

FISH AND SEA FOOD
LOS PESCADOS Y LOS MARISCOS

Crab Tostadas
Tostadas de Cangrejo 35

Garlic Shrimp
Camarones al Ajillo...284

Seafood Medley Shells Baked in a Butter, Garlic
    and Bacon Sauce
Conchas de Mariscos Horneadas en Salsa de
    Mantequilla, Ajo y Tocino 286

Shrimp Ceviche
Ceviche de Camarón..81

Red Snapper Ceviche
Ceviche de Huachinango 82

Tin Foil Baked Sea Bass in a Tequila-Chipotle Salsa
Filete de Róbalo Empapelado en Salsa de Tequila y
    Chipotle..54

Tuna Fish or Octopus Ceviche
Ceviche de Atún o Pulpo 83

White Fish Baked in Sea Shells
Conchas de Pescado al Horno 52

BEEF, PORK AND POULTRY
LAS CARNES

Beef Filets in Avocado Tequila-Lime Sauce
Filete en Salsa de Aguacate al Tequila y Limón 285

Breaded Chicken Baguette
Tortas de Milanesa 183

Chicken and Ham Patties
Croquetas de pollo y Jamón 281

Chicken in Fig and Red Wine Sauce
Pollo en Salsa de Higos y Vino Rojo 276

Chicken Medallions in Assorted Mushroom
   and Chipotle Sauce
*Medallones de Pollo en salsa de Hongos
   y Chipotle* 274

Chicken Pieces in Cilantro Creamy Sauce
Trozos de Pollo en Salsa Cremosa de Cilantro 280

Doña Rosa's Pork Carnitas
Carnitas Doña Rosa 150

Filet Mignon in Peppercorn Sauce
Filete Mignon a la Pimienta Verde 270

Filet Tips Sautéed in Ancho-Pasilla Sauce
*Puntas de Filete en Salsa de Chiles Ancho
   y Pasilla* 272

Meatballs Stuffed with Potatoes and Chorizo
Albóndigas Rellenas de Papa y Chorizo 56

Pibil Chicken
Pollo Pibil 278

Pork Tenderloin in Sweet Red Wine and Roasted
   Garlic Sauce
*Lomo de Puerco en Salsa Dulce de Vino Rojo y Ajo
   Rostizado* 273

SALADS & VEGETARIAN DISHES
LAS ENSALADAS Y LOS PLATILLOS
VEGETARIANOS

Avocado Stuffed with Pork Rind Salad
Aguacate Relleno de Ensalada de Chicharrón 153

Aztec Salad
Ensalada Azteca 264

Cactus Salad
Ensalada de Nopalitos 72

Corn off the Cobb
Esquites 36

Green Bean and Tomato Salad with Balsamic
   Vinaigrette
*Ensalada de Ejotes y Jitomate con Vinagreta de
   Balsámico* 58

Honey-Cinnamon Sweet Potatoes
Camotes con Miel y Canela 60

Mexican-Style Potato Salad
Ensalada de Papa Estilo Mexicano 263

Mixed Green Salad with Walnuts and Fruits in a
   Pink Rose Vinaigrette
*Ensalada de Lechugas Mixtas, Nueces y Frutas con
   Aderezo de Rosas* 265

Pickled Chiles Poblanos and Vegetables
Chiles Poblanos y Verduritas en Escabeche 64

Pickled Poblano Chiles Stuffed with Mashed
   Avocado
Chiles Poblanos en Escabeche Rellenos de Aguacate .. 66

Potato Cakes
Tortitas de Papa 152

Sautéed Baby Potatoes
Papitas de Cambray 262

Seasonal Fruit Salad with Pecans in a Creamy
   Dressing
*Ensalada de Frutas de la Estación con Nueces y
   Aderezo de Crema* 156

Seasoned Scallions
Cebollitas...231

Shrimp Salad in Purple Cabbage Cups with
  Guava Dressing
Ensalada de Camarón en Copitas de Col Morada con
  Aderezo de Guayaba 266

Spinach Salad with Panela Cheese and Fried
  Tortilla Strips
Ensalada de Espinaca con Queso Panela y Tortillas
  Fritas 71

Surimi Crab Salad in Carved Cucumber Cups
Ensalada de Surimi en Copitas de Pepino............267

Tortilla Casserole
Pastel Azteca 74

Zucchini, Corn and Cheese Crêpes
Crepas Rellenas de Calabacitas, Elotes y Queso...282

Salsas
Las Salsas

Dried Chile Sauce with Beer
Salsa de Chiles Secos con Cerveza 239

Green Salsa Made in a Molcajete
Salsa Verde de Molcajete....................................245

Green Tomatillo Salsa with Avocado
Salsa Verde de Tomatillo con Aguacate 236

Pasilla Chile and Tequila Salsa
Salsa de Chile Pasilla y Tequila 222

Pico de Gallo
Salsa Mexicana 240

Raw Green Salsa
Salsa Verde Cruda...238

Red Salsa Made in a Molcajete
Salsa Roja de Molcajete.................................. 244

Roasted Green Tomatillo Salsa
Salsa de Tomatillos Verdes.................................237

Tomatillo and Chipotle Salsa
Salsa de Tomatillo y Chipotle.............................241

Tomato and Ancho Chile Salsa
Salsa de Jitomate y Chiles Anchos 242

Tropical Fruit Pico de Gallo
Pico de Gallo Tropical 243

Tacos
Los Tacos y Las Cazuelas

Beefsteak Tacos
Tacos de Bistec...219

Chicken in Tomato Sauce Tacos
Tacos de Pollo en Salsa de Jitomate 224

Fried Chorizo and Potato Tacos
Tacos Dorados de Chorizo y Papa 220

Pibil-Style Pulled Pork Tacos
Tacos de Cochinita Pibil 228

Poblano Peppers with Cream Tacos
Tacos de Rajas con Crema 230

Pork Rinds Cooked in Red Sauce Tacos
Tacos de Chicharrón en Salsa Roja 225

Shrimp Taquitos
Taquitos de Camarón 226

Sweet Ground Beef Tacos with a Pasilla Chile and
  Tequila Salsa
Tacos de Picadillo Dulce con Salsa de Chile Pasilla y
  Tequila 222

Taquitos Silao-Style
Taquitos de Silao...212

Rice
Arroz

Black Rice
Arroz Negro 254

Mexican Pink Rice
Arroz Rosa Mexicano.......................................257

Mexican-Style Rice
Arroz a la Mexicana 251

Rice with Vanilla, Fried Mashed Bananas, Raisins, and Rum
Arroz con Vainilla, Plátanos Fritos Machacados, Pasitas y Ron 258

White Rice Cups Topped with Cactus Salad
Copitas de Arroz Blanco con Ensalada de Nopalitos 252

ARTISAN ICE-CREAMS AND SHERBETS
LAS NIEVES Y LOS HELADOS CASEROS

Avocado Ice-Cream
Helado de Aguacate 194

Corn Ice-Cream
Helado de Elote 197

Creamy 'Pasta de Salamanca' Sherbet
Nieve de Pasta de Salamanca 199

Farmers Cheese with Raisins and Tequila Ice-Cream
Helado de Queso Fresco con Pasitas y Tequila 192

Jícama and Pineapple Sherbets with Apricot – Lime Savory Chamoy Hot Sauce
Nieve de Jícama y Piña con Salsa de Chamoy Picante 204

Lemon and Key Lime Sherbet
Nieve de Lima y Limón 200

Mango Sherbet with Chile Powder
Nieve de Mango y Chile Piquin 203

Mexican Chocolate Ice-Cream
Helado de Chocolate Mexicano 190

Peanut Ice-Cream
Helado de Cacahuate 196

Prickly Pear Sherbet
Nieve de Tuna 201

Rice Pudding Ice-Cream
Helado de Arroz con Leche 198

Watermelon and Tequila Ice
Granita de Sandía y Tequila 206

DESSERTS AND CANDIES
LOS POSTRES Y LOS DULCES

Alfeñiques (mold required)
Alfeñiques (con moldes 114

Alfeñiques (no mold required)
Alfeñiques (sin moldes 113

Banana Crêpes with Mexican Chocolate Sauce
Crepas de Plátano con Salsa de Chocolate Mexicano 296

Burnt Milk with Prune Compote
Leche Quemada con Compota de Ciruela 294

Candied Pumpkin
Calabaza en Tacha 122

Churros
Churros 124

Corn Cake with Strawberry Syrup
Pastel de Elote con Jarabe de Fresas 100

Cream Custard with Milk Caramel
Natilla de Cajeta 292

Crystalized Limes with Coconut Candy Filling
Limones Cristalizados Rellenos de Dulce de Coco 168

Crystalized Sweet Potatoes
Camote Cristalizado 170

Curdled Milk Dessert
Chongos Zamoranos 158

Grandma Flora's Chocolate Mousse
Mousse de Chocolate de la Abuela Flora 59

Lime Dessert
Postre de Limón 298

Margarita Mousse
Mousse de Margarita 302

Mexican Coconut Candy
Cocada de Leche 172

Mexican Wedding Cakes
Polvorones 305

Milk and Pecan Candy
Jamoncillo de Nuez 310

Milk Caramel Crêpes with Chopped Pecans and
    Mangoes Flambé
Crepas de Cajeta con Nueces Picadas y Mangos
    Flameados 102

Pecan Crème
Crema de Nuez 291

Rice Pudding
Arroz con Leche 76

Simple Meringue with Vanilla Whipped Cream
    and Wild Berries
Merengues con Crema de Vainilla
    y Moras Silvestres 308

Strawberry Wrapped Baby
Niño Envuelto de Fresa 300

Strawberries with Fresh Cream
Fresas con Crema 210

Sylvia's Apple Pie
Pay de Manzana Sylvia 78

Three Milks and Milk Caramel Jell-o with
    Kahlúa Sauce
Gelatina de Tres Leches y Cajeta
    con Salsa de Kahlúa 306

Triple Sec Flan with Caramel-Orange Sauce
Flan de Triple Sec con Salsa de
    Caramelo y Naranja 312

Vanilla Milk Caramel from Celaya
Cajeta de Vainilla de Celaya 208

Yam Candy Bars from Puebla
Camote de Puebla 304

Acknowledgements:

Sylvia Kurian, Diana Anhalt, Nedda Anhalt, Carra Stratton, Patrick Anhalt, Daniella Gitlin, Enrique Gitlin, Nicole Gitlin, Nathaniel Lanzer, Lisa Tucker, Eugenia Meyer, Paula Rosner, Fina Ickowicz, Carrie Christie, Carmen Godoy-Covarrubias, Antonio Gálvez, Laura Carballo, Georgina Landa (Bindya), Carly Cross, Beverly Barry, Sarah Grzeskowiak, Robert Barrends, James Rusk, Faye MacClellan, Nadia Pizzaro, Fabrizio Cretella, Román Amezcua, Christian Reitler, Mark Spence, and Christa Glennie-Saychew.

With deepest gratitude to our book designing team, *the*BookDesigners: Ian Shimkoviak, Alan Hebel, and Billy Bjorncrantz.

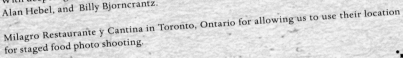

Milagro Restaurante y Cantina in Toronto, Ontario for allowing us to use their location for staged food photo shooting.